THE AGE OF TERROR

THE AGE OF

John Lewis Gaddis

Abbas Amanat

Paul Kennedy

Charles Hill

Niall Ferguson

Harold Hongju Koh

Paul Bracken

Maxine Singer

TERROR

America and the World
After September 11

EDITED BY
STROBE TALBOTT
AND NAYAN CHANDA

BASIC
BOOKS

A MEMBER OF THE
PERSEUS BOOKS GROUP

YALE CENTER FOR THE STUDY OF GLOBALIZATION

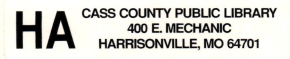

CONTENTS

INTRODUCTION

M OMENTOUS EVENTS HAVE a way of connecting individuals both to history and to one another. So it was on September 11. Even before more than 4,000 people died in less than two hours, there were farewell messages from the sky. In their last minutes, doomed passengers used cell phones to reach loved ones. A short time later, office workers trapped high in the burning towers called spouses, children, parents. Never had so many had the means to say good-bye.

During the hours afterward, the survivors scrambled to make contact with family and friends. "Are you all right?" they asked.

After the intimate connections came the communal ones—in religious observances, town meetings, hastily arranged get-togethers in places of work, television and radio call-in shows. There were gatherings at schools and colleges across the United States. At Yale, where six of the authors of the following essays teach, the first assembly was pastoral, reserved for prayer and moments of silence.

As the enormity of it all began to sink in, the question hanging in the air was, Were *we* all right?

"We" meant more than Americans. The list of the victims in New York was as cosmopolitan as the city itself. There were citizens of 62 countries, including 250 Indians, 200 Pakistanis, 200 Britons, 55 Australians and 23 Japanese. On every continent, places of worship held memorial services; parks and squares filled with people demonstrating their sympathy; thousands lined up at U.S. embassies and consulates to sign condolence books. There were two large candlelight vigils in Iran. Americans were inundated with phone calls, emails and letters with messages of empathy from abroad.

Partly, no doubt, because of this outpouring of compassion, support and solidarity from around the world, the isolationist nerve in the American body politic barely twitched. There was a surge of combative patriotism, but it left room for variations on the theme *we're all in this thing together*. In his address to the joint houses of Congress, President Bush made a point of internationalizing the nation's sense of outrage and resolve: "This is the world's fight. This is civilization's fight."

In the weeks that followed, students everywhere wanted to keep getting together, not just for solace and reflection but for inquiry into what had happened, who had done it, why, what it meant, and what the U.S. and others should do about it. What they'd witnessed, many of them said, cried out for context.

"Teach-in," the phrase from the sixties and seventies, didn't quite apply, since the teachers didn't have many answers, or even all the right questions. They knew it. September 11, like the commandeered planes themselves, had come out of the blue. Just as the U.S. government was caught off guard, so the citizenry was unprepared, emotionally and intellectually.

In discussions around the Yale campus—in classrooms, common rooms and dining halls, at kitchen tables in faculty homes, on lawns in the sunshine throughout an especially mild and glorious Indian summer—a number of us noted a humbling irony: the more time we'd spent in the old world and the better we thought we understood its organizing principles, the less ready we were for the new one. Not surprisingly, therefore, it was often from the students—who had just experienced the first great public trauma of their lives— that we heard an especially useful insight, a fresh intuition or a clarifying formulation of one of the many ethical, political and strategic tests that lay ahead.

Suddenly, familiar terms and concepts were inadequate, starting with the word terrorism itself. The dictionary defines it as violence, particularly against civilians, carried out for a political purpose. September 11 certainly qualified. But America's earlier encounters with terrorism neither anticipated nor encompassed this new manifestation. U.S. citizens had been casualties before, but usually when they were far from home—in a military barracks in Lebanon in 1983 or Saudi Arabia in 1996, on a cruise ship in the Mediterranean in 1985, in a jumbo jet over Scotland in 1988, or in two U.S. embassies in East Africa in 1998. This time, the prey were not just on American soil but inside the iconic headquarters of American prosperity, security and strength.

September 11 left nearly five times as many Americans dead as all terrorist incidents of the previous three decades combined. The carnage was nearly thirty times greater than what Timothy McVeigh, a homegrown madman, had inflicted on Oklahoma City in 1995, and about double what three hundred Japanese bombers left in their wake at Pearl Harbor. Commentators instantly evoked that other bolt-from-the-blue raid, sixty years before, as the closest thing to a precedent. But there really was none. This was something new under the sun.

The attacks were immediately declared acts of war. Yet that word, too, seemed not quite to fit. We'd always thought of war either as civil strife within a nation or systematic violence committed by one state or alliance against another. War, however brutal and capricious, had its own rules and made its own accommodations, even in the midst of mayhem, with the human instinct for self-preservation. While risking death and meting it out to others, combatants hoped to survive and savor victory. The cold war never turned hot because the superpowers agreed on one thing if nothing else—the overarching imperative of avoiding Armageddon.

This new enemy was different. Osama bin Laden's organization, al Qaeda, flew no flag—it was the ultimate NGO—and his warriors seemed inspired rather than deterred by the prospect of their own fiery deaths.

What was it, exactly, that inspired them? Part of the answer, undeniably, had something to do with one of the world's great religions and the spiritual home of several great civilizations. The pilots, whose names and mug shots people all over the world came to know well, were driven not just by anger and hatred but by a grotesque yet, for them at least, compelling version of the Muslim faith. Many Americans who had never seen a copy of the Koran, much less read a single passage, were riveted by the last will and testament of Mohammed Atta, who was probably at the controls of American Flight 11 when it slammed into the north tower of the World Trade Center at 8:45 a.m. That document was perhaps deliberately left behind in a piece of luggage so that it could be excerpted in newspapers all over the world. It was filled with exhortations to martyrdom and promises of divine reward for the eighteen other hijackers. Those for whom Atta's letter was an introduction to the teachings of the Prophet went from knowing little about Islam to thinking they now knew quite a bit.

Some Muslim clerics and scholars spoke out promptly and eloquently, denouncing Atta's beliefs, like his actions, as abomination. But many others in the Muslim world reacted to the horror with a sullen and knowing silence (the unstated message: "We always said you'd reap the whirlwind!"), or with denial ("This crime has nothing to do with religion!"), or with invidious comparisons (equating the deliberate slaughter of thousands of innocents with Israel's selective assassination of Palestinian radicals and its police and military actions to contain and suppress the uprising in the occupied territories).

Another word that figured prominently in the aftermath of September 11 was globalization. The editors of this book came to Yale last summer to establish a center devoted to the study of how the interplay of economies, cultures, societies and political systems is changing the world. We had just begun our first staff meeting of the academic year when a colleague interrupted with the news from New York. Globalization had already been a source of confusion and a subject of controversy. It had its boosters, its critics and its violent opponents. Now, in bin Laden, globalization had an archenemy who was also, in lethally effective ways, a master of its tools and techniques.

The terrorists attacked the nation that, more than any other, had both driven globalization and benefited from it. They did so largely for that reason—that is, among their targets was globalization itself. The phenomenon is, in its essence, about breaking down barriers and bridging divides. Bin Laden and his accomplices were bent on burning bridges and building walls, figuratively and literally. Globalization is about integration and inclusion; their aim was partition and expulsion.

Bin Laden also succeeded, for the moment at least, in reversing what many had hoped would be the benevolent dynamic of globalization. The revolution over the last thirty years in communication and transportation has empowered individuals, making it possible for them to move money, products, information and ideas across borders in ways that previously had been the monopoly of governments and giant corporations. The terrorists took full advantage of that freedom and harnessed it to their cause. Claiming to be champions of the powerless masses of the earth, they found a way of attacking the most powerful state. They designed a mode of assault that, in jujitsu fashion, turned core American strengths—openness and mobility—into vulnerabilities. They dispatched the hijackers, armed with the most low-tech weapons imaginable (box cutters), to ride one of the emblematic technologies of the modern world, the passenger jet, from the periphery—that is, those lands where many feel like globalization's losers—to the center, where the winners were beginning another workday.

It was mass murder as performance art. The staging and timing guaranteed maximum coverage worldwide. On the day the American and British reprisals began, the invisible impresario, bin Laden, made a virtual appearance by means of a pretaped statement for television that would be broadcast repeatedly for days afterward, putting his own spin on footage of the skies lighting up over Kabul. Then he disappeared back into his cave to oversee Act II. Within weeks microscopic spores of *Bacillus anthracis*—sender unknown—began showing up in the U.S. mail.

It was with the onslaught of bioterrorism in early October that an anxiety became a certainty: September 11 had been just the beginning. People everywhere would have to get used to being afraid in ways and to a degree that they had never known before. It was in that sense that the U.S. had entered an age of terror.

The evil that befell the U.S. was absolute. It triggered a natural impulse for a reciprocally absolute doctrine. President Bush provided one: *If you harbor terrorists, you're a terrorist; if you aid and abet terrorists, you're a terrorist—and you will be treated as one.*

Quickly, however, it became clear that both the problem and the solution were more complicated. Good versus evil was a template that had worked for wars in the past (most notably, the Allies versus the Axis in World War II), but in this new struggle, the question of which side everyone was on risked some awkward answers. For example, Saudi Arabia—bin Laden's estranged homeland—had, for decades, paid what amounted to protection money to Islamic extremists and obscurantists. Without Saudi indulgence and, in earlier ventures, direct Saudi support, bin Laden would never have become a household word. Did that make Saudi Arabia our enemy or our friend? The short answer was neither.

Al Qaeda and the Taliban regime were also discomfiting case studies in the perils of expediency. These two entities, now on the receiving end of American bombs and cruise missiles, were incubated in the U.S.'s proxy war against the Soviets in Afghanistan in the 1980s. Not for the first time, nor for the last, U.S. foreign policy followed an old adage of Eastern *realpolitik*: the enemy of my enemy is my friend. In the nineties, some of those friends had turned into the worst of enemies. And now, in America's new war against its old allies of convenience, the U.S. was in the market for new ones—anyone who was prepared to sign up to counter-terrorism as an overarching imperative.

Again, the vocabulary contains its own traps. The truism that one person's terrorist is another's freedom fighter (which sets teeth on edge in some circles and heads nodding in others) has a corollary: one person's counterterrorist is another's ethnic cleanser. Minorities that have long been suppressed or brutalized by central authorities, such as the Chechens in Russia and the Uighurs in China, had reason to worry about a new wave of crackdowns post-September 11, only this time with less protest on their behalf from the outside world.

In striking against targets nearly 7,000 miles away from his Afghan lair, part of bin Laden's intention was to stir up populations closer to home—and to stir them up not just against the Great Satan, but against their own repressive, corrupt, frightened rulers as well. In addition to the twin towers in Lower Manhattan, the terrorists were trying to bring down two other less sturdy edifices, the pro-Western military regime in Pakistan and the House of Saud. The attack was a classic provocation: an attempt to goad the U.S. into lashing out far and wide, throughout the Arab world and the Gulf, thus turning the public in those countries against the powers that be, local and global.

The U.S. and its coalition partners saw this danger and did their best to calibrate the nature and scope of their military action accordingly. But every passing day provided a fresh reminder that bin Laden had, in addition to a far-flung network of assassins, a broad and eclectic constituency for which "evildoers" did not suit as a blanket label. The second shock for many Americans on September 11 was the spectacle—doted on by Western television coverage—of young Palestinians dancing and cheering in the streets. In the days and weeks that followed, the talking heads on television included Egyptian intellectuals who professed disapproval of the attacks but whose more heartfelt message seemed to be that the U.S. had this coming. By October, news stories appeared about a fad among Pakistani mothers to name their newborn sons Osama.

To regard these people as no better than the terrorists themselves would be to concede a major point to bin Laden. He was trying to give new impetus to the polarization of the world. If he had a motto, it was that we're *not* all in this thing together. For him, it was believers (and believers only in his version of Islam) versus infidels. He was the self-proclaimed messiah of what might yet turn out to be the self-fulfilling prophecy of the clash of civilizations. The challenge was to make sure he failed in that respect, as in all others.

In pondering this and the other dilemmas that burst into our lives on September 11, a knowledge of history helped.

Clear thinking about what lies ahead means, among other things, rethinking what has gone before, since there was obviously plenty that we had misunderstood or missed altogether. Otherwise the U.S. and the world would have been ready for September 11. Or more to the point, through concerted action, the world might even have kept it from happening. Hence the participation in this book of four historians along with a career diplomat, a professor of law, a political scientist and a molecular biologist.

John Lewis Gaddis asserts that the collapse of the World Trade Center towers will prove to be as consequential as the fall of the Berlin Wall twelve years earlier. He finds in the U.S. conduct of the cold war and its nameless sequel ("the post-cold war era") guidelines for waging the struggle ahead. Paul Kennedy appraises the long-term prospects for American power and offers his view on how to maintain it in the face of a new menace that applies guerrilla tactics on a global scale. Abbas Amanat traces the roots of Islamic extremism to the Muslim experience with colonialism and its aftermath, as well as to the Iranian revolution's anti-American passions and its celebration of martyrdom. Charles Hill puts the onus for the instability in the Middle East on the backward and autocratic ruling structures in the region, and on what he believes to be a decade of American vacillation and neglect. Niall Ferguson assesses America's role as the sole economic and military superpower—a mature empire facing a crucial test of its will and leadership—and asks the question, "Do the leaders of the one

state with the economic resources to make the world a better place have the guts to do it?" Harold Hongju Koh sees
September 11 as a test of America's commitment to democracy, rule of law and human rights, both at home and
abroad. Paul Bracken focuses on the failure of the U.S.
intelligence and defense establishments, urging that the new
Office of Homeland Security adopt some of the management techniques of corporate America to fix a system that
was broken even before September 11. Maxine Singer looks
back to an earlier Bush—Franklin Roosevelt's science
adviser Vannevar Bush—for a model of how the U.S. should
mobilize the nation's scientific, technological and medical
expertise to battle bioterrorism and other hazards that
come out of petri dishes, test tubes and—the ultimate
nightmare—nuclear laboratories.

In assembling these essays, it was our working premise that
the unforgivable is not necessarily incomprehensible or inex-
plicable. Comprehension and explanation are what the
authors—seven teachers and a scientist—do for a living, and
it's what they do here. They have offered both more and less
than conclusions. The pace, complexity and unpredictability
of events render inconclusive any judgments or prescriptions
in a book that went to press in early November, it appeared
that no matter what the immediate outcome of the war in
Afghanistan, the struggle in its many dimensions would continue for a long time. The purpose here is to capture how, in
the first month and a half after September 11, eight minds
grappled with what happened that day, and what each of

them believes are the principal lessons, goals and caveats that should guide us as we recover. Recovery means that when we—all of us, the world over—eventually answer the question "Are we all right?" the answer will be yes.

—Nayan Chanda and Strobe Talbott
November 1, 2001
New Haven, Connecticut

THE AUTHORS

ABBAS AMANAT is a professor of history and chair of the Council on Middle East Studies at Yale. He was born in Iran and educated at Tehran and Oxford Universities. Among his writings are studies of apocalypticism in modern Islam and the history of American diplomacy in the Middle East. He is currently working on a history of modern Iran.

PAUL BRACKEN is a professor of management and political science at Yale. His most recent book is *Fire in the East: The Rise of Asian Military Power and the Second Nuclear Age*, and he is now writing a book on new challenges to American military power.

NIALL FERGUSON is a professor of political and financial history at the University of Oxford and a visiting professor of economics at the Stern School of Business,

New York University. He is a prolific commentator on contemporary politics, and the author of several books, including *The Pity of War* and *The Cash Nexus: Money and Power in the Modern World, 1700–2000*. He is currently working on a history of the British Empire and its lessons for America today.

J O H N L E W I S G A D D I S is a professor of history at Yale and a senior fellow of the Hoover Institution at Stanford. He has taught at Ohio University, the Naval War College, the University of Helsinki, Princeton and Oxford. His most recent book is *We Now Know: Rethinking Cold War History*. He is working on a biography of George F. Kennan.

C H A R L E S H I L L is a distinguished fellow in international security studies at Yale and affiliated with the Hoover Institution and Baylor University as well. A career diplomat in the U.S. Foreign Service, he served in various posts in Washington and abroad relating to China and the Middle East. He was an aide to Secretaries of State Kissinger, Haig and Shultz, and a special adviser to United Nations Secretary-General Boutros Boutros-Ghali.

P A U L K E N N E D Y is professor of history and director of International Security Studies at Yale. Born in England and educated at Oxford, he is the author of thirteen books, including *The Rise and Fall of the Great Powers*. He is currently writing two books, on the evolution of ideas about the United Nations and on international affairs in the twentieth century.

HAROLD HONGJU KOH is professor of international law at Yale. He served as Assistant Secretary of State for Democracy, Human Rights, and Labor in the Clinton administration. He is currently writing a book entitled *Why Nations Obey: A Theory of Compliance with International Law.*

MAXINE SINGER is a molecular biologist and president of the Carnegie Institution of Washington, which conducts research in biology, astronomy, and earth and planetary sciences. She was a researcher for more than thirty years at the National Institutes of Health. She is a member of the National Academy of Sciences and chairman of its Committee on Science, Engineering, and Public Policy.

The Editors

NAYAN CHANDA is the director of publications at the Yale Center for the Study of Globalization. He was editor and editor-at-large of the *Far Eastern Economic Review* from 1996 until 2001, and for twenty-two years before that he was a correspondent of the magazine. He is the author of *Brother Enemy: The War After the War* and coauthor of over a dozen books on Asian politics, security and foreign policy.

STROBE TALBOTT is the director of the Yale Center for the Study of Globalization. He was Deputy Secretary of State from 1994 until 2001. Before joining government, he was a journalist for twenty-one years at *Time* magazine. The author of six books on arms control and U.S.–Soviet relations and *The Russia Hand: A Memoir of Presidential Diplomacy*, to be published in the spring.

CHAPTER I

AND NOW THIS: LESSONS FROM THE OLD ERA FOR THE NEW ONE

John Lewis Gaddis

W E ' V E N E V E R H A D a good name for it, and now it's over. The post-cold war era—let us call it that for want of any better term—began with the collapse of one structure, the Berlin Wall on November 9, 1989, and ended with the collapse of another, the World Trade Center's twin towers on September 11, 2001. No one, apart from the few people who plotted and carried out these events, could have anticipated that they were going to happen. But from the moment they did happen, everyone acknowledged that everything had changed.

It's characteristic of such turning points that they shed more light on the history that preceded them than on what's to come. The fall of the Berlin Wall didn't tell us much about the post-cold war world, but it told us a lot about the cold war. It suddenly became clear that East Germany, the Warsaw Pact, and the Soviet Union itself had long since lost the authority with which the U.S. and its NATO allies had continued to credit them right up to the day the wall came down. The whole history of the cold war looked different as a result. Having witnessed the end, historians could never again see the middle, or even the beginning, as they once had.

Something similar seems likely to happen now to the post-cold war era. For whatever we eventually settle on calling the events of September 11—the Attack on America, Black Tuesday, 9/11—they've already forced a reconsideration, not only of where we are as a nation and where we may be going, but also of where we've been, even of who we are. Our recent past, all at once, has been thrown into sharp relief, even as our future remains obscure. To paraphrase an old prayer, it's obvious now that we have done some things which we ought not to have done, and that we have not done other things which we ought to have done. How much health there is in us will depend, to a considerable degree, on how we sort this out.

I.

But first things first. No acts of commission or omission by the U.S. can have justified what happened on September 11. Few if any moral standards have deeper roots than the prohibition against taking innocent life in peacetime. Whatever differences may exist in culture, religion, race, class, or any of the other categories by which human beings seek to establish their identities, this rule transcends them.

The September 11 attacks violated it in ways that go well beyond all other terrorist attacks in the past: first by the absence of any stated cause to be served; second by the failure to provide warning; and finally by the obvious intent to time and configure the attack in such a manner as to take as many lives as possible—even to the point, some have suggested, of the airplanes' angle of approach, which seemed calculated to devastate as many floors of the twin towers as they could. Let there be no mistake: this was evil, and no set of grievances real or imagined, however strongly felt or widely held, can excuse it.

At the same time, though, neither our outrage nor the patriotic unity that is arising from it relieves us of the obligation to think critically. Would anyone claim, in the aftermath of September 11, that the U.S. can continue the policies it was following with respect to its national defense or toward the world before September 11? Americans were not *responsible* for what happened at Pearl Harbor; but they would have been *irresponsible* in the extreme if they had not, as a consequence of that attack, dramatically altered their policies. Nobody—given the opportunity to rerun the events leading up to that catastrophe—would have handled things again in just the same way.

It's in that spirit, I think, that we need a reconsideration of how the U.S. has managed its responsibilities in the decade since the cold war ended, not with a view to assigning blame, indulging in recrimination, or wallowing in self-pity, but rather for the purpose—now urgent—of determining where we go from here. Patriotism demands nothing less.

2.

The clearest conclusion to emerge from the events of September 11 is that *the geographical position and the military power of the U.S. are no longer sufficient to ensure its security.*

Americans have known insecurity before in their home-land, but not for a very long time. Except for Pearl Harbor and a few isolated pinpricks like Japanese attempts to start forest fires with incendiary bombs in the Pacific Northwest in 1942, or the Mexican guerrilla leader Pancho Villa's raid on Columbus, New Mexico, in 1916, the U.S. has suffered no foreign attack on its soil since British troops captured Washington and burned the White House and the Capitol in 1814. There's a macabre symmetry in the possibility that the fourth plane hijacked on September 11—which crashed pre-sumably after an uprising among the passengers—probably had one of these buildings as its target.

Few other nations have worried so little for so long about what is coming to be called "homeland security." The late Yale historian C. Vann Woodward even went so far as to define this lack of concern as a central feature of the American character. "Free security," he insisted, had done as much to shape Americans' view of themselves as had the availability of free, or almost free, land.

The 20th century, to be sure, eroded that sense of safety, but this happened as a result of the larger role the U.S. had assigned itself in world affairs, together with ominous shifts in the European balance of power. It did not arise from any sense of domestic insecurity. We entered World War I to ensure that Germany did not wind up dominating Europe, and we were preparing to do the same thing again in World War II when the Japanese attack, followed by Hitler's own declaration of war, removed any choice in the matter from us.

Even so, the continental U.S. remained secure throughout the long and bloody conflict that followed. Neither the Germans nor the Japanese could bomb our cities or occupy our territory, as we eventually would do to them. And despite the incarceration of some 120,000 Japanese Americans during the war, the only significant fifth-column network operating within the U.S. at the time was that of an ally, the Soviet Union—a fact not discovered until after the war had ended. The world might be unsafe, but homeland security could be taken for granted almost as easily during the total wars of the 20th century as it had been throughout most of the 19th century.

The cold war made the American homeland seem less secure in two ways: when spies working on behalf of the Soviet Union were shown to have betrayed the country; and as the prospect arose that Soviet long-range bombers and later intercontinental ballistic missiles might soon be capable of reaching American soil. The spies were mostly rounded up by the time McCarthyism reached its peak in the early 1950s, a fact that helps to account for why that season of paranoia went away as quickly as it did. The nuclear danger never entirely went away, and for a while it was a palpable presence for Americans who saw their public buildings designated as fallout shelters even as they were being encouraged, for a while, to build their own in their own backyards.

Despite moments of genuine fear, however, as during the Berlin and Cuban missile crises, the only images we had of destroyed American cities were those constructed by the makers of apocalypse films and the authors of science fiction novels. Real danger remained remote. We had adversaries, but we also had the means of deterring them.

Even cold war insecurities, therefore, never meant that Americans, while living, working and traveling within their country, had to fear for their lives. Dangers to the American homeland were always vague and distant, however clear and present overseas dangers may have been. The very term "national security," invented during World War II and put to such frequent use during the cold war, always implied that both threats and vulnerabilities lay *outside* the country. Our military and intelligence forces were configured accordingly.

That's why the U.S. Commission on National Security in the 21st Century—often known, for its co-chairs Gary Hart and Warren Rudman, as the Hart-Rudman Report—distinguished between "national" and "homeland" security when it warned of our domestic vulnerabilities, with uncanny prescience, in March 2001. In the aftermath of September 11, we have not only adopted the concept of "homeland security"—it has become synonymous with national security. Such is the revolution in our thinking forced upon us by the events of that day. It means that Americans have entered a new stage in their history in which they can no longer take security for granted: it is no longer free—anywhere, or at any time.

What was striking about September 11 was the success with which the terrorists transformed objects we had never before regarded as dangerous into weapons of lethal potency. There was nothing exotic here like bombs or even firearms. They used instead the objects of everyday life: pocket knives, twine, box-cutters and, of course, commercial aircraft. The terrorists also combined what may seem to us to be a primitive belief in the rewards of martyrdom with the most modern methods of planning, coordination, and execution. We confront, therefore, not only a new category of easily available weaponry, but a new combination of skill and will in using it.

The attack's cost-effectiveness was equally striking. No previous act of terrorism came close to this one in lives lost and damage inflicted. The dead were almost twice the number killed in some three decades of violence in Northern Ireland. They are ten times the toll on both sides in the most recent round of the Israeli-Palestinian *intifada*. They exceed, in deaths suffered on a single day, the most violent battles of the American Civil War. The operation required the lives of nineteen terrorists and expenditures of about $500,000. The "payoff," if we can use such a term for such a brutal transaction, was approximately 5,000 dead and perhaps as much as $100 billion in recovery costs. Ratios like these—some 263 victims for every terrorist, and $2,000 in damages for every dollar expended—cannot help but set a standard to which future terrorists will aspire.

The whole point of terrorism is leverage: to accomplish a lot with a little. This operation, in that sense, succeeded brilliantly—even allowing for the fact that one of the four planes failed to reach its target, and that more planes may have been in danger of being hijacked. As a consequence, the images of terrified New Yorkers running through the streets of their city to escape great billowing clouds of ash, dust, and building fragments; or of the government in Washington forced to seek shelter; or of several days of skies devoid of the contrails we have come to expect aircraft to add to the atmosphere over our heads—these memories will remain in our minds just as vividly as the images, from six decades earlier, of American naval vessels aflame, sinking at their own docks within an American naval base on American territory.

Security, therefore, has a new meaning, for which little in our history and even less in our planning has prepared us.

3.

That leads to a second conclusion, which is *that our foreign policy since the cold war ended has insufficiently served our interests.*

National security requires more than just military deployments or intelligence operations. It depends ultimately upon creating an international environment congenial to the nation's interests. That's the role of foreign policy. Despite many mistakes and diversions along the way, the U.S. managed to build such an environment during the second half of the 20th century. The Soviet Union's collapse stemmed, in no small measure, from its failure to do the same.

As a consequence, the world at the end of the cold war was closer to a consensus in favor of American values—collective security, democracy, capitalism—than it had ever been before. President George H. W. Bush's talk of a "new world order" reflected a convergence of interests among the great powers which, while imperfect, was nonetheless unprecedented. Differences remained with the European Union, Russia, China and Japan over such issues as international trade, the handling of regional conflicts, the management of national economies, the definition and hence the protection of human rights; but these were minor compared to issues that had produced two world wars and perpetuated the cold war. Americans, it seemed, had finally found a congenial world.

What's happened since, though? Can anyone claim that the world of 2001—even before September 11—was as friendly to American interests as it had been in 1991? It would be silly to blame the U.S. alone for the disappoint-ments of the past decade. Too many other actors, ranging from Saddam Hussein to Slobodan Milosevic to Osama bin Laden, have helped to bring them about. But the question that haunted Americans after Pearl Harbor is still worth ask-ing: given the opportunity to rerun the sequence, what would we want to change in our foreign policy and what would we leave the same?

The question is not at all hypothetical. The administration of George W. Bush has already undertaken, in the wake of September 11, the most sweeping reassessment of foreign policy priorities since the cold war ended. Its results are not yet clear, but the tilt is far more toward change than continu-ity. That is an implicit acknowledgment of deficiencies in the American approach to the world during the post–cold war era that are clearer now than they were then.

One of these, it seems, was unilateralism, an occupational hazard of sole surviving superpowers. With so little coun-tervailing power in sight, such states tend to lead without listening, a habit that can cause resistance even among those otherwise disposed to follow. The U.S. managed to avoid this outcome after its victory in World War II because we had, in the Soviet Union, a superpower competitor. Our allies, and even our former adversaries, tolerated a certain amount of arrogance on our part because there was always "something worse" out there; we in turn, fearing their defection or collapse, treated them with greater deference and respect than they might have expected given the power imbalances of the time.

With our victory in the cold war, though, we lost the "something worse." American ideas, institutions, and culture remained as attractive as ever throughout much of the world, but American policies began to come across as overbearing, self-indulgent, and insensitive to the interests of others. Our own domestic politics made things worse: with the White House in the control of one party and the Congress in the hands of another during most of this period, it was difficult to get a consensus on such matters as paying United Nations dues, participating in the International Criminal Court, or ratifying the Comprehensive Test Ban Treaty, the Land Mines Convention, or the Kyoto Protocol on Climate Change. During most of the cold war, knowing what our enemies would make of our failure to do these things, it would have been easy.

A second problem arose, largely as a result of this unilateralism: we neglected the cultivation of great power relationships. We seemed to have assumed, perhaps because we were the greatest of the great powers, that we no longer needed the cooperation of the others to promote our interests. We therefore allowed our relations with the Russians and the Chinese to deteriorate to the point that by the end of that decade we were barely on speaking terms with Moscow and Beijing. We failed to sustain one of the most remarkable achievements of American foreign policy during the cold war—the success of Richard Nixon and Henry Kissinger in creating a situation in which our adversaries feared one another more than they feared us. It was as if we had switched our source of geopolitical inspiration from Otto von Bismarck to the Kaiser Wilhelm II.

This happened chiefly as the result of a third characteristic of our post-cold war foreign policy, which was a preference for justice at the expense of order. We had never entirely neglected the demands of justice during the cold war, but we did tend to pursue these by working with the powerful to get them to improve their treatment of the powerless. We sought to promote human rights from the inside out rather than from the outside in: sometimes we succeeded, sometimes we did not.

With the end of the cold war, however, we changed our approach. We enlarged NATO against the wishes of the Russians, not because the Poles, the Czechs, and the Hungarians added significantly to the alliance's military capabilities, but rather because these states had suffered past injustices and therefore "deserved" membership. We then used the expanded alliance to rescue the Kosovars and bomb the Serbs, despite the fact that in doing so we were violating the sovereignty of an internationally recognized state without explicit United Nations approval. Unsurprisingly, this angered not just the Russians but also the Chinese, both of whom had discontented minorities of their own to worry about. Our intentions were praiseworthy in both of these episodes; but our attention to their larger geopolitical implications was not what it might have been.

A fourth aspect of our post-cold war foreign policy followed from the third: it was the inconsistency with which we pursued regional justice. We were, as it turned out, by no means as adamant in seeking justice for the Chechens or the Tibetans as we were for the Kosovars: Moscow and Beijing, despite their nervousness, had little to fear. But by applying universal principles on a less than universal basis, Washington did open itself to the charge of hypocrisy. It was worse elsewhere, as in Somalia, where our reluctance to take casualties of our own revealed how little we were prepared to sacrifice for the rights of others, or in Rwanda, where we responded to the greatest atrocities of the decade by simply averting our eyes.

Meanwhile, in the Middle East, we tolerated the continuing Israeli dispossession and repression of Palestinians even as we were seeking to secure the rights of the Palestinians; and we did nothing to adjust policy in response to the fact that an old adversary, Iran, was moving toward free elections and a parliamentary system even as old allies like Saudi Arabia were shunning such innovations. There was, in short, a gap between our principles and our practices: we proclaimed the former without linking them to the latter, and that invited disillusionment. There are several reasons why the rantings of bin Laden resonate to the extent that they do in so many parts of North Africa, the Middle East, and Asia; but surely this is one of them.

A fifth problem was our tendency to regard our economic system as a model to be applied throughout the rest of the world, without regard to differences in local conditions and with little sense of the effects it would have in generating inequality. The problem was particularly evident in Russia, where we too easily assumed a smooth transition to market capitalism. Our efforts to help came nowhere near the scope and seriousness of the programs we'd launched to rebuild the economies of our defeated adversaries after World War II.

Meanwhile, Washington officials were less sensitive than they should have been to the extent to which American wealth and power were being blamed, throughout much of the world, for the inequities the globalization of capitalism was generating. Capitalism would have expanded after the cold war regardless of what the U.S. did. By linking that expansion so explicitly with our foreign policy objectives, however, we associated ourselves with something abroad that we would never have tolerated at home: the workings of an unregulated market devoid of a social safety net. Adam Smith was right in claiming that the pursuit of self-interest ultimately benefits the collective interest; but Karl Marx was right when he pointed out that wealth is not distributed to everyone equally at the same time, and that alienation arises as a result. The U.S. and most other advanced societies found ways to reconcile these competing truths with the emergence of the regulatory state during the first half of the 20th century: capitalism might not have survived had that not happened. No such reconciliation was sought, however, as a foreign policy priority during the post–cold war era.

Finally, and largely as a consequence, the U.S. emphasized

the advantages, while neglecting the dangers, of globalization. There was a great deal of talk after the cold war ended
of the extent to which that process had blurred the boundary
between the domestic and the international: it was held to be
a good thing that capital, commodities, ideas and people
could move more freely across boundaries. There was little
talk, though, of an alternative possibility: that danger might
move just as freely. That's a major lesson of September 11:
the very instruments of the new world order—airplanes, liberal policies on immigration and money transfers, multicul-
turalism itself in the sense that there seemed nothing odd
about the hijackers when they were taking their flight training—can be turned horribly against it. It was as if we had
convinced ourselves that the new world of global communication had somehow transformed an old aspect of human
nature, which is the tendency to harbor grievances and
sometimes to act upon them.

What connects these shortcomings is a failure of strategic
vision: the ability to see how the parts of one's policy combine to form the whole. This means avoiding the illusion that
one can pursue particular policies in particular places without their interacting with one another. It means remembering that actions have consequences: that for every action
there will be a reaction, the nature of which won't always be
predictable. It means accepting the fact that there's not always
a linear relationship between input and output: that vast
efforts can produce minimal results in some situations, and
that minimal efforts can produce vast consequences in oth-

ers. It means thinking about the implications of such asymmetries for the relationship between ends and means, always the central problem of strategy: leverage is important, and our adversaries have so far proven more successful than we in using it. Finally, it requires effective national leadership, a quality for which American foreign policy during the post-cold war era is unlikely to be remembered.

So what might we have done differently in the realm of foreign policy? Quite a lot, it's now clear, as we look back on a decade in which it appears that our power exceeded our wisdom.

4.

Where do we go from here? Will the events of September 11 bring our policies back into line with our interests? Can we regain the clarity of strategic vision that served us well during the cold war, and that seemed to desert us during its aftermath? Shocks like this do have the advantage of concentrating the mind. Those of us who worried, during the 1990s, about the difficulty of thinking strategically in an age of apparent safety need no longer do so. As was the case with Pearl Harbor, a confusing world has suddenly become less so, even if at horrendous cost.

What's emerging is the prospect, once again, of "something worse" than an American-dominated world—perhaps something much worse. The appalling nature of the attacks on New York and Washington forged a new coalition against

terrorism overnight. The great power consensus that with-
ered after 1991 is back in place in expanded form: the U.S.,
the European Union, Russia, China and Japan are all on the
same side now—at least on the issue of terrorism—and
they've been joined by unexpected allies like Pakistan,
Uzbekistan, and perhaps even, very discreetly, Iran. Terrorism
can hardly flourish without some state support; but
September 11 brought home the fact that terrorism challenges the authority of all states. Everybody has airplanes, and
everything that lies below them must now be considered a
potential target. Just as fear of the Soviet Union built and
sustained an American coalition during the cold war—and
just the prospect of nuclear annihilation caused the Soviets
themselves ultimately to begin cooperating with it—so the
sudden appearance of "something much worse" is a paradoxical but powerful ally in the new war that now confronts us.

Maintaining this coalition, however, will require tolerating
diversity within it. That was one of our strengths during the
cold war: the U.S. was far more successful than the Soviet
Union in leading while listening, so that those we led felt
that they had an interest in being led. NATO survived, as a
consequence, while the Sino-Soviet alliance and the Warsaw
Pact did not. If the global coalition against terrorism is to
survive, it will demand even greater flexibility on the part of
Americans than our cold war coalition did. We'll have to give
up the unilateralism we indulged in during the post-cold war
era: the Bush administration, prior to September 11, had
seemed particularly to relish this bad habit. We'll have to

define our allies more in terms of shared interests, and less in terms of shared values. We'll have to compromise more than we might like in promoting human rights, open markets, and the scrupulous observance of democratic procedures. We'll have to concentrate more than we have in the past on getting whatever help we can in the war against terrorism wherever we can find it. Our concerns with regional justice may suffer as a result: we're not likely to return soon to rescuing Kosovars, or to condemning oppression against Chechens and Tibetans. The compensation, one hopes, will be to secure justice on a broader scale; for terrorism will offer little justice for anyone.

Even as we pursue this path, we'll need to address the grievances that fuel terrorism in the first place. Once again, there are cold war precedents: with the rehabilitation of Germany and Japan after World War II, together with the Marshall Plan, we fought the conditions that made the Soviet alternative attractive even as we sought to contain the Soviets themselves. We launched our own form of asymmetrical warfare against communism. Our "leverage" was to deploy our strengths imaginatively against its weaknesses, and the "payoff" was easily as disproportionate as anything the terrorists achieved on September 11. A relatively small investment of resources and intelligence secured for the U.S. and its allies, during the second half of the 20th century, a far more congenial world than what they had had to live through during its first half. Can we apply the same strategy now against the conditions that breed terrorists in so many parts of what we used to call the "third" world? We'd better try, for some of these regions are at least as much at risk now as Europe and Japan were half a century ago.

The era we've just entered—whatever we decide to call it—is bound to be more painful than the one we've just left. The antiterrorist coalition is sure to undergo strains as its priorities shift from recovery to retaliation. Defections will doubtless occur. Further terrorist attacks are unavoidable, and are certain to produce demoralization as well as greater resolve.

But it does seem likely, even at this early stage in the war they have provoked, that the terrorists have got more than they bargained for. "What kind of a people do they think we are?" Winston Churchill asked of the Japanese in the aftermath of Pearl Harbor. It's worth asking the same of our new enemies, because *it can hardly have been their purpose to give the U.S. yet another chance to lead the world into a new era, together with the opportunity to do it, this time, more wisely.*

CHAPTER 2

EMPOWERED THROUGH VIOLENCE: THE REINVENTING OF ISLAMIC EXTREMISM

Abbas Amanat

I T REMAINS A telling feature of September 11 that no
individual or group explicitly claimed responsibility. The
perpetrators, suicides and survivors alike, stopped short of
confessing their crime or taking credit for the heroic blow
they felt they had struck against the symbols of America's
financial and military power. It is as though they wanted the
terror and carnage to speak for themselves. When a taped
interview of Osama bin Laden ran on television on October
7, the day U.S. and British air strikes began against targets in
Afghanistan, bin Laden confined himself to praising the martyrs for thrusting the "sword of Islam" into the U.S. as punishment for American and Israeli occupation of the Islamic
holy lands.

To this author, a historian of the Middle East who grew
up in that part of the world, bin Laden's message of violence
comes as a sobering reminder of what has become of the

Middle East. This is not only because an outrage of unprecedented magnitude has been committed by some Middle Easterners against the U.S., which is both demonized in that region and seductive to many who live there. Nor is it because such an act confirmed the worst stereotypes of violence and fanaticism long associated with Islam and the Middle East. It was also because the outrage revealed much about the undeniable and alarming growth of religious extremism in the Muslim world, a trend that has been deeply intertwined with the tortured historical experience of becoming modern.

There is an admirable effort in the U.S. and in other Western societies to differentiate between extremism and mainstream Islamic beliefs and practices. The presence of many Muslim communities in the West has itself had an educational and salutary effect. All of us, I expect—whatever our own backgrounds and perspectives—would like to believe that bin Laden, along with his al Qaeda network, is a grotesque anomaly. If we could believe that, we would feel safer, and it would augur well for dialogue, and coexistence, between Muslim and non-Muslim cultures and societies. But this latest manifestation of Islamic extremism cannot be seen in isolation from wider and deeper problems, both in the Middle East itself and at the core of Western—and American—policy toward that region.

In seeking a historical context for the upsurge of militancy, one may draw not just from the tradition of rational observation, so much esteemed in the West, but also from the

Koran's repeated appeals to reason. The once-thriving tradition of humanism and receptivity to other cultures in the Islamic world could also serve as a point of departure. Ironically, the land that today is Afghanistan, now one of the unhappiest and most brutalized countries in the world, once witnessed a brilliant and mutually enriching interplay of civilizations. It was there that Persian and Buddhist cultures came together to give birth to a humanistic tradition of coexistence. Later, Herat, which figured prominently on the target list of American bombers last fall, was, in the 15th century, the center of a burst of cultural creativity in the arts, literature, architecture and science comparable in its sweep and in the quality of its achievements to the Renaissance that was under way in southern Europe around the same time. In symbolic contrast, last spring the Taliban, in a glaring display of bigotry and ignorance, destroyed the magnificent carved effigies of the Buddha in the ancient city of Bamian in central Afghanistan.

In coming to terms with this contrast, we cannot but view the phenomenon of the Taliban as the final outcome of a structural fault in the very shaping of Afghanistan. The European colonial powers of the 19th century, along with the superpowers of the 20th, have much to answer for. The rules of the Great Game, as the rivalry between Russia and Britain was labeled, demanded the reshaping of Afghanistan as a buffer. But that meant trying to carve out a new country that was fragmented by language, ethnicity, tribal allegiances, religious creed, geography, and historical and cultural experience. The outcome never fully submitted to the will of the colonial powers, nor was it ever fully integrated as a modern nation state. And when, in the late 20th century, these structural faults gave way under the weight of rival ideologies and were exposed to the vagaries of the superpower rivalry, the strict and angry Islam of the Taliban emerged as the only force that could hold Afghanistan together. In this respect Afghanistan mirrored the painful story of much of the postcolonial Muslim world, reflecting the extremes of religious militancy that looms over the horizon of so many Muslim societies.

I.

The emergence of the construct we call Islamic extremism, with its penchant for defiance, resentment, and violence, has its roots in the history of the Muslim sense of decline and its unhappy encounter with the dominant West. It is sobering to remind ourselves how frequently the Middle East, as one part of the Muslim world, has been visited by waves of violence in its recent history. Since the end of the Second World War, the area extending from Egypt and Turkey in the west to Afghanistan in the northwest and Yemen in the south has suffered at least ten major wars—and that's not counting the U.S. engagement in Afghanistan after September 11. Casualties have run into millions. Populations have been uprooted, societies torn up by their roots, political structures demolished—all on a massive scale. Three of the region's wars were fought with Western powers (Britain's and France's attacks on Egypt during the Suez crisis in 1956; the Soviet Union's long, losing effort to subjugate Afghanistan in the 1980s; the American-led campaign to liberate Kuwait from Iraq in 1990-91); Israel and its Arab neighbors waged five wars (1948, 1956, 1967, 1973 and 1982); Yemen and Lebanon have suffered prolonged civil wars; and Iraq and Iran fought for eight years. The transforming effects of these crises haunted the last several generations in the Middle East. Throughout the region people have become ever more disillusioned with the deeply-entrenched dictatorships in their own countries, with the collapse of democratic institutions, hollow nationalistic rhetoric, and with their failing economies.

In the minds of many, Western powers shared the blame, both directly and indirectly. Whether based on historical reality or faulty perception, holding the Western powers responsible made special sense against the backdrop of a powerful West and a powerless Middle East. From the days of the European colonial powers in the 19th century to the more recent interventions of the superpowers, there has been a pattern of diplomatic, military and economic presence tying the fate of the Middle East and its resources to the West. Whether motivated by oil, grand strategy or support for Israel, the Western powers were either involved in, or perceived to be behind, most of the region's political crises.

As a result, for new generations of Middle Easterners perceptions of the West, and particularly of the U.S., dramatically changed for the worse. Long gone were the images of well-wishing Yankees who established schools, universities and hospitals, distributed food, and supported nationalist endeavors. Instead, fascination with a luster of American popular culture was only heightened thanks to Hollywood and American high tech—computers, video games, and satellite dishes. Yet in a paradoxical turn, as the lines of visa-seekers in front of U.S. consulates grew longer, a cloud of mistrust and resentment against the U.S. also settled over the region. The people in the Middle East began to view American society through the lenses of sitcoms and softwares. To many unaccustomed eyes, the U.S. seemed like the center of a greedy, materialistic and uncaring world obsessed with violence and promiscuity. The U.S.'s unreserved support for Israel, its backing of unpopular regimes, and its fighter jets over Middle Eastern skies only added to anti-American feelings.

2.

Mistrust toward the West deepened as a result of the problematic way the Middle East improvised its own version of modernity. Since the beginning of the 20th century, Westernization has transformed lifestyles and expectations. Yet, despite an undeniable measure of growth and material improvement, today's Middle East by most economic indicators is still one of the least developed regions in the world. It is grappling endlessly with failed centralized planning, high birthrates, lopsided distribution of wealth, high unemployment, widespread corruption, inefficient bureaucracies, and environmental and health problems. The frustration endemic among the young urban classes—often the children of rural migrants who came to the cities in search of a better life and a higher income—is a response to these conundrums.

For the population of the Middle East, progressively younger because of high birthrates, uprooted from their traditional setting, and deprived of illusive privileges that they can see around them and on television screens but cannot have, the familiar and comforting space of Islam offers a welcoming alternative. Daily prayers, Friday sermons, Koranic study groups, Islamic charities—these are all part of that space. But so are the street demonstrations and the clandestine pamphlets, with their fiery anti-establishment, anti-secular, and anti-Zionist message.

In dealing with these restive multitudes, the governments of the Middle East and their associated ruling elites have little to offer. They are themselves part of the problem as they contribute to the public perception of powerlessness. In the period right after World War II, nationalist ideologies were highly effective in mobilizing the public against the European colonial presence. But over time they often hindered the growth of democratic institutions and the emergence of an enduring civil society. The army officers who came to power in Egypt, Syria, Iraq, and elsewhere through military coups, and prolonged their leadership through repressive means, invested heavily in anti-Western rhetoric. Yet facing the erosion of their own legitimacy, they learned to pay a lip service to the rising Islamic sentiments in their societies, exploiting them as a cushion between the elite and the masses and to suppress individual freedoms.

The predictable victims of this appeasement were the modernizing urban middle classes of the Middle East. Though small and vulnerable, these middle classes were crucial conduits for modernizing even as they preserved a sense of national culture. Egypt, Iraq, Syria, Turkey, and Iran, in their rush for an illusive economic growth, and greater equity, purposely undermined the economic bases of their middle classes. They did so through heavy-handed state planning and the mindless nationalization programs. The middle classes in the Middle East today, besieged and intimidated, are no longer willing or able to take up the cause of democratic reforms. They have instead given rise to a spoiled crust of the politically silenced and submissive class whose voice of protest is heard, increasingly, through extremist causes.

Out of this milieu came Mohamed Atta, a failed son of an affluent Egyptian lawyer. Another example is bin Laden's chief lieutenant, Ayman al-Zawahiri, a physician from a celebrated Egyptian family.

This staggering reorientation toward radical Islam needs to be understood in light of a deeper crisis of identity in the Arab world. In the post-colonial period, most nation-states in that region had to improvise their own ideologies of territorial nationalism in order to hold together what were often disjointed local and ethnic identities. At the same time they had to remain loyal to the ideology of pan-Arabism—the notion, or dream, that all Arab peoples make up one super-nation—a project that was destined to fail dismally. Egypt came out of the colonial experience with what might have been the basis for its own Egyptian nationalism, but under Gamal Abdel Nasser, it traded that away for leadership of the pan-Arab cause. Yet the experiences of secular pan-Arabism, whether that of the Nasser era in the 1950s and 60s or the Ba'thist regimes of Iraq and Syria in the 1960s and 1970s, proved illusory to the intellectuals who championed it. It was even more unrewarding to the Arab masses who for decades were exposed to the state-run propaganda machines and to the often demagogic street politics. The harsh realities of the military and paramilitary regimes of the Arab world sobered even the most ardent supporters of Arab nationalism.

It was in this environment of despair that the disempowered Arab masses came to share the common cause of confronting Zionism. Resistance to the establishment of the Jewish homeland since the end of World War I and to the creation of the state of Israel in 1947 offered the Arab world a rallying point of great symbolic power. The subsequent experiences of multiple defeats in wars against Israel revived in the Arab psyche memories of prolonged colonial domination. From the Arab nationalist perspective, Zionism was not merely another form of imagined nationalism rooted in the 19th century, but a project designed by the West to perpetuate its imperial presence and protect its vested interests in the region—the latest manifestation of centuries of enmity against the Muslim peoples. For many in the Arab world it was comforting to believe that the reason why hundreds of millions of Arabs could not defeat Israel was because Western powers were protecting it. And more often than not there was ample evidence to convince them of the validity of their claim.

3.

Not surprisingly, the sense of despair toward repressive regimes at home and helplessness against the consolidation of the neighboring Zionist state engendered a new spirit of Islamic solidarity. It was radical in its politics, monolithic in its approach, and defiant toward the West.

The decisive shift came not inside the Arab world but with the 1979 revolution in Iran. The establishment of an Islamic republic under the leadership of the uncompromising Ayatollah Khomeini evoked throughout the Muslim world the long-cherished desire for creating a genuine Islamic regime. Even though it was preached by a radical Shi'a clergy who committed enormous atrocities against his own people, the Iranian model of revolutionary Islam was viewed as pointing the way to an "authentic" and universalist Islam. Through cassette tapes and demonstrations, Iranian revolutionaries managed to topple the Shah and the mighty Pahlavi regime despite its vast military arsenal, secularizing program, and Western backing. Even more empowering was the revolution's anti-imperialist rhetoric.

After his followers besieged the American embassy and held its staff hostage in 1980-81, Khomeini labeled the U.S. as the Great Satan for backing the "Pharaonic" powers—a label for the shah and conservative rulers elsewhere in the region—and for repressing the "disinherited" of the earth.

The Iraq-Iran War of 1980-88 further established the appeal of the paradigm of martyrdom that had long been deeply rooted in Shi'a Islam. That conflict was portrayed as an apocalyptic jihad between the forces of truth and falsehood. In addition to defending their own nation, the Iranians believed they were exporting their revolution. As the slogan on the banners declared and as the battle cries of many teenage volunteers confirmed, the path of Islamic liberation stretched across the battlefields to the Shi'a holy cities of Karbala' and Najaf in Iraq all the way to Jerusalem.

Even if the Iranian revolution failed to take root elsewhere, the celebration of martyrdom found resonance far and wide. The revolutionary Shiites of Lebanon's Hezbollah, and later the young Palestinians who eagerly volunteered for suicide bombings on behalf of the Hamas and Islamic Jihad, saw martyrdom as a way of empowerment. It is not difficult to see the same traits among the hijackers of September 11.

The accelerated pace of Islamic radicalism in the early 1980s, whether inspired by the Iranian revolution or reacting to it, helped shape the outlook of a generation from which came the extremism of Osama bin Laden himself. In his twenties, he was a pious, though uninspiring, student in Jidda University in Saudi Arabia. He came from a superrich family with close connections to the Saudi royalty. In November 1979, he must have witnessed the siege of the Grand Mosque of Mecca and the revolt under the leadership of a messianic figure who claimed to have received direct authority from the Prophet to render justice. The quick suppression of this revolt by the Saudi authorities came only a month after the signing of the Camp David peace agreement between Israel and Egypt. The treaty was received by the Islamic activists throughout the Arab world as a betrayal to the Arab and Islamic causes. Only a year later, in October 1980, the Egyptian president, Anwar al-Sadat, was assassinated by a splinter group of the Muslim Brothers with Ayman al-Zawahiri, bin Laden's future lieutenant, was associated.

The Mecca uprising and Sadat's assassination were both inspired by a tradition of religious radicalism going back to the Society of the Muslim Brothers in the 1920s and 30s and before that to the Wahhabi movement that began in the late 18th century. The central doctrine of Wahhabism was a return to the way of "virtuous ancestors," a highly regressive, monolithic interpretation of Islam known as Salafiyya, a doctrinal propensity that for centuries encouraged strict adherence to puritanical principles.

In the early 20th century, the Salafiyya played a central part in the shaping of Saudi Arabia as an Islamic state. It also served as the guiding doctrine for the Muslim Brother's goal of moral and political reconstruction. Inspired by the ideas of Sayyid Qutb, a leader of the Muslim Brothers—who was executed in 1966 by the Nasser regime—this ideology received a new lease on life. A true believer was required to "renounce" the dark sacrilege of his secular surroundings. The primary targets were the regimes of the Arab world, whose secularism was labeled a return to the "paganism" of pre-Islamic times. Qutb urged the Muslim Brothers to follow the model of the Prophet and seek refuge in the safety of an isolated space. This exhortation was a call on believers to reenact the Hijra (immigration), in which the Prophet left the Mecca of the pagans and traveled to Medina. That moment marked the beginning of the Islamic calendar and history.

The doctrine of Salafiyya and its articulation by Sayyid Qutb gained an overwhelming currency among Islamic radicals in the early 1980s. But the wilderness that might serve as a refuge for them could not be recreated in the oil-rich Saudi Arabia of bin Laden or in the tourist-infested Egypt of al-Zawahiri. Instead, Afghanistan beckoned. The burgeoning resistance movement against the occupying Soviet forces there was highly appealing to radical and moderate sentiments alike. It could unite activists of all Islamic persuasions for a common cause of fighting the spread of the godless communism. Moreover, taking up the cause of the Afghan mujahideen against the Soviets helped boost the prestige of the Saudi regime both in the eyes of Muslims and in the eyes of the U.S., which was determined to prevent Moscow's advances toward the Persian Gulf.

In the decade following the Soviet invasion of Afghanistan in late 1979, Saudi public and private funds, along with covert U.S. training and military support, backed the mujahideen's war. Contributing to this effort, the Pakistani army provided the logistical support, and Wahhabi-oriented religious schools in Peshawar—the Pakistani frontier town at the foot of the Khyber Pass—guaranteed a steady flow of fervent Islamic missionaries and fierce, devout fighters for the battle under way against the occupiers of the "Evil Empire" in Afghanistan. To add even more of an Islamic flavor to the quarrelsome Afghan resistance, the CIA also sought from the Saudi kingdom the token presence of one of the pious members of the royal family.

4.

Osama bin Laden, the fervent, charismatic volunteer, was more credible and effective than a reluctant and aging Saudi prince. Bin Laden enjoyed the political and financial backing of many conservative donors. A looming figure at six-foot-six, clad in those days in Savile Row suits, he arrived in Peshawar in the mid-1980s. There he soon found himself at odds with the fiercely factional mujahideen who spoke not Arabic but Pashtu and Dari (a dialect of Persian). Still fewer shared bin Laden's devotion to militant Wahhabism. Over time, however, he found refuge in a clique of like-minded volunteers who soon came to be known as the Arab Afghans. What held together this growing international brigade, perhaps as many as five thousand, was a sense of Arab camaraderie in the loneliness of a strange land. They were renegades and self-exiles from all over the Arab world, from Morocco to Yemen, many of them with a record of religious militancy at home.

In the shelter of his headquarters, bin Laden and his cohorts developed their plan to lay the ground for a universalist Islamic state, if necessary through the use of violence. His program for an Islamic state, as articulated over the next few years, claimed a theocratic over-lordship of the Arab and the Islamic world, reviving the classical Islamic notion of the Caliphate.

In Peshawar, bin Laden's mentors included Abdullah Azzam, a radical Jordanian Palestinian who was killed in a car bomb in 1989, and Abdul Rasul Sayyaf, a militant Wahhabi preacher dispatched by the Saudi authorities to serve as the ideological proconsul to the Afghan mujahideen. The inglorious defeat of the Soviet forces added to bin Laden's prestige in Afghanistan and within the Islamic world generally, even though the contribution of the Arab Afghans to the struggle was marginal and came late in the game. It was as the Soviets were withdrawing that bin Laden founded al Qaeda—literally, "the base"—a cluster of military-ideological camps. The principal aim was to spread Wahhabism among the Afghans, but that effort met with little success. Al-Qaeda quickly became a refuge for the remnants of the Arab Afghans and their families and, in keeping with its name, a base of operations elsewhere.

In the early 1990s bin Laden became something of a wanderer. The chaotic scramble that followed the collapse of the pro-Soviet regime and that eventually brought the bickering Afghan mujahideen to Kabul in 1992 disillusioned him, since the Hekmatyar faction—the most radical of the mujahideen backed by bin Laden—did not come to power. He returned for a while to Saudi Arabia, then moved to Sudan, where a militant Islamic regime had come to power.

The major turning point for bin Laden however came with the Gulf War. At the outset of Saddam Hussein's occupation of Kuwait, bin Laden proposed to launch a jihad against Iraq, but he was turned down by the Saudi authorities, who found him an embarrassing nuisance. Bin Laden's disapproval of the American intervention turned into open hostility with the stationing of a large contingent of U.S. troops on Saudi soil. He viewed as contrary to the strict teachings of Wahhabi Islam a non-Muslim military presence in the Arabian peninsula. It is likely that he was also bitter about the U.S. abandonment of the Afghan mujahideen after the Soviet withdrawal.

Whatever the source of bin Laden's personal grudge and doctrinal antipathy toward the U.S., he had at his disposal a growing pool of anti-American extremism from which to draw as he assembled his networks. The outcome of the Persian Gulf War confirmed in many eyes a grave paradox in the conduct of American foreign policy. The U.S. was seen as mustering a grand coalition against Iraq for the sake of its own national interests, and in particular the safe and continuous flow of oil. The issue of protecting the territorial integrity of Kuwait thus seemed brazenly hypocritical to those who contrasted it with the U.S.'s deliberate disregard for Israel's prolonged occupation of the Palestinian territories. In the eyes of the critics, the U.S.'s decision not to pursue the war beyond Kuwait was seen as further proof of a self-serving and shortsighted policy. It allowed Saddam Hussein to crush the revolts against him inside Iraq while imposing debilitating sanctions on the people of Iraq, practically partitioning the country yet leaving his tyranny in place.

Bin Laden's personal odyssey further affirmed his anti-American resolve. In 1994, under American pressure, the Saudi authorities revoked his passport and froze his assets. Two years later Washington succeeded in pressuring Sudan to deny him the safe haven he had enjoyed there. As a last resort he sought refuge with the Taliban, who had taken control of Kabul in 1996, in exchange for his financial and logistic support.

The Taliban was the other side of the al Qaeda coin. The Wahhabi propaganda campaign, which went on under Saudi auspices for at least two decades, was the chief factor behind the emergence of this militant student movement that eventually took over Afghanistan. In the 1980s and 90s through patronage and missionary work, financing the construction of new communal mosques from Indonesia and the

Philippines to sub-Saharan Africa and Central Asia, training young students of many nationalities in pro-Wahhabi subsidized seminaries, making available to the public the Wahhabi literature, establishing interest-free charity and scholarships for the poor, facilitating the transfer of the Hajj pilgrims, and backing conservative clerical elements with Wahhabi proclivities, the Saudi establishment built a strong and growing network that is now changing the face of Islam throughout the towns and villages of the Muslim world. Inadvertently, this network proved to be a fertile ground for garnering support for bin Laden from Pakistan and southern Afghanistan to Central Asia, Africa and Southeast Asia.

The Taliban movement took root among the dislocated and deprived children of the Afghan refugees trained in the religious schools of Pakistan financed by private Saudi funding. Armed with Wahhabi fervor for jihad and little else, under the auspices of the Pakistani army intelligence these seminarians were organized into a fighting force. The political lacuna that came about as a result of the devastating Afghan civil war opened the way for the Taliban's gradual advance and eventual takeover. The regime they established embodied all the neo-Wahhabi zeal that was preached in the Peshawar schools. It revived and imposed a strict patriarchal order deeply hostile to women and their education and public presence. It allowed battering, even killing, of women by their male relatives, enforced facial veiling, and closed most girl's schools. It displayed extraordinary intolerance toward Shiites and other minorities, obliterated even the most primitive symbols of a modern culture, and undermined all human and individual rights. In the name of purging Afghanistan of factionalism and ending the civil war, the Taliban turned it into a miserable fortress whose people suffered from starvation and isolation.

In the year that bin Laden arrived in Afghanistan, he issued a fatwa, or religious ruling, that called upon all Muslims to kill Americans as a religious duty. The 1998 bombing of the American embassies in Nairobi and Dar es Salaam was, as far as we know, his first attempt to put his own ruling into practice. This came at the time when al Qaeda's merger with Egyptian Islamic Jihad—led by Ayman al-Zawahiri, who had recently masterminded the killing of fifty-eight tourists in Luxor, Egypt—and other terrorist organizations drastically increased bin Laden's capacity to wreak havoc. The U.S. tried to punish him for the embassy bombings by firing missiles into his camps. His emerging unscathed gave him greater confidence and enhanced his reputation for invincibility in the eyes of his followers.

For bin Laden and his al Qaeda associates, the terrorist war against the U.S. was a struggle rooted in Islam's noble past and ensured of victory by God. In this context, the attack on giant structures representing American economic and military might was a largely symbolic act that would, they hoped, miraculously subdue their enemies, just as the infidels of early Islam eventually succumbed to the Prophet's attacks on their caravans. This theory of terror, violent and

indiscriminate, though utterly against the mainstream interpretation of Islam, attracted a small but committed group of
devotees who also saw self-sacrifice as a permissible avenue
toward symbolic achievement of their goals.

In several respects, however, bin Laden's apocalyptic vision
was grounded in reality and geared to the possible. He and
his associates were men of worldly capabilities who could
employ business administration models to generate revenue,
invest capital in the market, create a disciplined leadership,
recruit volunteers, incorporate other extremist groups,
organize and maintain new cells, issue orders and communi-
cate through a franchised network of semi-autonomous units
on a global scale. This mix of the messianic and the pragmatic allowed al Qaeda to tailor its rhetoric to the grievances of
its growing audience and to carry out recruitment and
indoctrination on a wider scale.

The vast majority of Muslims do not approve of bin
Laden's terrorism, nor do they share his ambition to build a
monolithic community based on a pan-Islamic order. Yet
there is an undeniable sympathy for the way he has manipulated grievances and symbols. The contrasting images of the
"pagan" America and the "authentic" Islam find currency in
wide and diverse quarters. One example is the young boys
among Afghan and Pakistani refugees who were brain-
washed in the Saudi-funded Wahhabi seminaries of
Peshawar—and from whose ranks rose the Taliban (the word
itself means "students"). Another is the new generation of

Western-educated Arab middle classes who were recruited to the al Qaeda's suicide cells in Europe.

We can read in the testament of Mohamed Atta, the Egyptian ringleader of the September 11 attacks, the typical obsessive enthusiasm of a born-again Muslim. As a reward for his resort to massive terror and destruction, which he carried out with resolve and precision, Atta seeks the Koranic promise of heavenly recompense especially reserved for martyrs. His literal reading of the sacred text is imbued with sexual references. "Know," he promises his accomplices, "that the gardens of paradise are waiting for you in all their beauty. And the women of paradise are waiting, calling out, 'Come hither, friends of God.' They are dressed in their most beautiful clothing." This is all the more glaring, and perversely pathetic, when contrasted with Atta's final encounters in a Florida strip club. One can only imagine that he was gazing at the barely-clad strippers of this world in anticipation of the houris—beautiful maidens awaiting the brave and virtuous—in paradise. This was the reward he expected for his martyrdom in the "battle for the sake of God," which he was waging, as he himself reminded us, in the "way of the pious forefathers." This surreal mix of the pious and the profane, backed by a litany of Koranic verses, reveals a discomfiting pseudomodern crust over the hard core of extremism.

As for bin Laden himself, he came into the spotlight after September 11 having shrouded himself and his cause in an apocalyptic aura. His October 7 statement broadcast on tele-

vision, both in tone and content, alluded to a seminal narra-
tive of Islam. Above all, he said, he placed his total trust in
God as he waged the struggle of true believers against infidels,
confident of the ultimate reward of martyrdom. His references to the impending fall of the "hypocrites"—those
Muslim individuals and governments who were not support-
ive of his cause—and to the sure victory of the righteous on
horseback and armed with swords—presumably in contrast to
the sophisticated weaponry of his enemies—all have resonance in the encoded story of early Islam. In a statement at
the same time, bin Laden's chief lieutenant, al-Zawahiri,
referred to the catastrophic loss of Muslim Spain at the end of
the 15th century. This, too, was meant to remind Muslims of
the greater days of Islam before its defeat by Christianity,
hence complementing bin Laden's vision of the glorious past.

5.

That al Qaeda effectively communicates to a wide audience
far beyond its own extremist circle there can be no doubt. In
doing so, it has found abundant opportunities, thanks to the
global media, and thanks to complacency and ignorance of
Western intelligence services and law enforcement agencies.
The dilemmas and inconsistencies of U.S. foreign policy in
the region also provided al Qaeda with its weapons of choice
to appeal to the frustration and anger of the mainstream
Muslims worldwide.

At the core of the resentment so widespread in the Arab and Islamic world is Israel and its treatment of the Palestinians in the occupied territories. Hundreds of millions of Arabs, and increasingly other Muslims as well, are now more than ever informed through media about the Palestinians' unending confrontations with the Israeli security forces. The scenes of stone-throwing youth in the face of Israeli live bullets, destruction of Palestinian houses, mourning and funeral processions, strikes and shop closures, roadblocks and humiliating searches, closures of the territories, the strangled Palestinian economy and growing poverty, and the rubble-ridden refugee camps all contrast with the newly-constructed and clean Israeli settlements built on usurped Palestinian orchards. The defiance of Jewish settlers, the arrogance of the Israeli politicians, the tanks, helicopter gunships, and jet fighters roaring overhead, the night raids, the detentions and frequent breaches of basic human rights—all these provoke intense sentiments of anger and frustration. Broadcast through the Arab networks, and more recently on the global al-Jazeerah television network based in Qatar—the outlet of choice for bin Laden himself—these tragic depictions are increasingly intermingled with symbols of Islamic defiance: the suicidal missions of Hamas and Islamic Jihad against Israeli targets, the fiery anti-American and anti-Israeli slogans and sermons in Friday congregations. Added to this is the enormous level of Islamic radical pamphleteering with anti-American and anti-Zionist content, not infrequently laced in the Arabic textbooks with flagrant anti-Jewish racial references.

The politically repressive regimes of most Arab countries permit anti-Zionist (and even anti-Jewish) expres-
sions as a safety valve. This further adds to the symbolic
value of the Palestinian cause as a powerful expression of
Arab unity with growing Islamic coloring. Since the
Intifada of 1986 and the 1993 Oslo Peace Accord, the
thrust of Arab public opinion has been directed toward the
fate of the Palestinians in the occupied territories rather
than against the very existence of Israel. Yet the oppressive
Arab regimes still use the hypocritical rhetoric of national
security as an impediment to the growth of democracy in
their own countries. In such a repressive environment the
mosque often functions as a political forum. There the differentiation between Israeli conduct and American foreign
policy fades. Arab public opinion widely believes that the
Jewish lobby in the U.S. is the sole determinant of
American policy in the region and therefore makes little
distinction between U.S. foreign policy and Israeli abuse of
the Palestinians.

Proponents of Muslim piety also hold American "corrupt-
ing influences" responsible for the erosion of the assumed
"authentic" mores of Islamic austerity and devotion. These
influences are widely associated with the worst clichés of
American popular culture and lifestyle. In this world of mis-
perceptions, the globally permeating images of promiscuity,
ostentatious wealth, organized crime, random violence, drug
use, gluttony and wastefulness contrast sharply with the ide-
alized Islamic virtues of moral outrage, self-sacrifice, other-

worldliness, brotherhood, and piety. The extremists eagerly and skillfully sell these contrasts to the ill-informed Muslim masses, who more than ever now rely on visual images thanks to the power of the electronic media.

To Muslim viewers around the world these exaggerated contrasts offer an elusive comfort, since they seem to explain the root cause of the perceived malfunction of their own governments and societies. They are all the more suggestive because they are shrewdly tied up with the story of sufferings of the Palestinian people at the hands of the Israelis and those of the Iraqi people under U.S.-upheld sanctions. On top of that, they are constantly reminded of the "defiling" of the Islamic holy lands by the presence of American troops in Saudi Arabia.

Bin Laden is a master at exploiting these symbolic references. The U.S. and its Western allies have tried to convince the world, and especially the Muslim world, that the campaign against bin Laden and al Qaeda is not directed at Islam but at terrorism. However, that differentiation won't carry much weight in the minds of many Muslims so long as bin Laden, "dead or alive," has at his disposal such potent propaganda weapons. The issue is not only the danger that he or people like him will turn their extremist dream into a religious war between Islam and the West. Equally important is that they will provoke an escalating conflict between militant neo-Wahhabi Islam and the retreating forces and quavering voices of moderation and tolerance in the Muslim world. Bin Laden presents to much of his audience the image of a messianic prophet. Even if he is killed for his cause, he will, in their eyes, have died a martyr's death.

The military operation that started on October 7 will be judged in the light of its full array of longer-term and wide-ranging consequences rather than its immediate military success. If it harms civilians, destabilizes the region, fuels extremism, and polarizes Muslim public opinion, it will be seen as a grave failure. The U.S. has enough painful memories of aerial bombing and its consequences in Vietnam, Cambodia and Iraq to make one feel skeptical of the successful outcome of this operation. If, however, eliminating bin Laden and his network is feasible and—just as important, if it is followed by a sincere effort to address the acute problems of the region—only then we view military action as justifiable. This means finding an enduring and comprehensive solution to the political vacuum that is about to emerge in Afghanistan and finding remedies to the miseries that the people of this country have sustained over the past two decades in the hands of superpowers and their own vicious warlords and fanatics.

On a wider scale, and over the long term, the U.S. and its Western allies cannot avoid revisiting their overall current stance toward the Middle East and the Muslim world as a whole, with all their cultural complexities. It will be highly imprudent, even reckless, to treat the Middle East and neighboring Muslim societies, with a population of half a billion, merely in terms of their available energy resources and strategic value. As the sole remaining superpower and the direct beneficiary of these resources, the U.S. cannot shy away from its responsibilities to the welfare of this region. The experiences of the past half century have shown that the profound problems that September 11 has brought so starkly to light cannot be resolved merely through the use of military force, partisan diplomacy, and sustaining oppressive but pro-Western regimes. Because of its inherent vulnerability as an open society, the U.S. cannot afford to side unfairly with one party in a protracted and emotional dispute at the obvious expense of the other. Moreover, the very American democratic precepts of freedom of speech and popular representation and its guarantees for individual and civil liberties are in apparent contrast to a course of foreign policy that perpetuates repression and conflict. Such a course only provides Islamic extremism with a greater following and brings about further acts of violence.

As much as the national security specialists and champions of a stronger defense call for heightening the walls of security, it is unrealistic to believe that combating the global problem of terror and extremism can be achieved by creating a fortress America. The U.S. could only benefit from promoting the cause of democracy and open society in the Muslim world and encouraging voices of moderation, religious tolerance, and human rights, at least in those countries where it still musters influence. Fostering a sustained and prudent promotion of democratic institutions without jeopardizing the very stability of these societies, and allowing an endogenous democratic process to take shape, are the very parameters upon which American vital interests can be maintained. If on the other hand the U.S. and its Western allies insist on clinging to tattered models of security and continue to show military intervention without measured compassion, they are likely to pay dearly for the consequences of an undemocratic, unstable and impoverished Middle East ablaze with religious extremism, territorial disputes, and violent displays of frustration.

The societies of the Middle East are not as hopeless and hapless as they may seem. There are voices of coexistence, toleration and understanding. There are those who advocate accepting a world order based on integration, collaboration and friendship. For hopeful signs, one need look only to today's Iran—twenty years into a revolution that instituted a repressive Islamic regime. Despite consistent demands for autocratic conformity and religious indoctrination now, experiences in democracy are not extinct. The calls for open society, coexistence, and rule of law are more audible than ever. And despite the regime-sponsored slogan of "Death to America," enthusiasm for learning more about the West and about the U.S. is at its height. These are prospects that are not to be overlooked in the midst of responding to terrorist acts and searching for their perpetrators.

CHAPTER 3

MAINTAINING AMERICAN POWER: FROM INJURY TO RECOVERY

Paul Kennedy

T HE TERRORIST ATTACK of September 11 was so
destructive of American lives, property, and pride that it
was unsurprising to see this nation immediately turn to history, literature and religious texts in an attempt to give meaning to what was happening. References to Pearl Harbor or
the London Blitz, quotations from Churchill's speeches, lines
from Walt Whitman and W. H. Auden, and meditations on
just and unjust wars were all part of the country's symbolic
and linguistic effort at understanding, which is the first and
necessary step from injury to recovery.

Shortly after the attacks, I recalled a bittersweet poem by
Rudyard Kipling from a hundred years ago, when the
British Empire, then at its zenith, found itself humiliated and
bloodied in South Africa by a relatively small band of
Afrikaaner irregular troops. They appeared to the haughty
British to be scruffy, hairy-faced farmers, bitterly opposed to

late-Victorian "progress" and the trends toward what we today would call globalization: that is, the ever-growing integration of economies and societies because of new communications, newer trade and investment patterns, the transmissions of cultural images and messages, and the erosion of local and traditional ways of life in the face of powerful economic forces from abroad. One hundred years ago, the influence of the City of London—that is, the global capitalist system of which London was the undisputed center—protected as it was by the global reach of the British army and navy, was as hated by the strongly puritan Boer farmers as the dominance of Wall Street and the Pentagon is to fanatical Muslims today.

It was easy for the British to scorn the Afrikaaners' backwardness and religious prejudices, but much less easy to crush their mobile commandos or kill their leaders. In fact, it took over 300,000 Empire troops three years to regain the upper hand, and the whole thing had a cathartic effect on British society, politics, and strategy. "We have had no end of a lesson," Kipling intoned in his poem. British military forces were not well equipped for guerrilla warfare, having been prepared for either the classic clash of European armies on the battlefield or suicidal attacks by dervishes against their regimental machine guns. Intelligence was lacking. Mobility and logistics were poor once the British troops were on the ground. The economy was hurt. Recovery was painful and led to a lot of hard questions and, in due course, military and administrative reforms.

History is replete with examples of well-established nations that received a staggering blow but then scrambled to recover from the wound. The Prussian state was brought to its knees at the hands of Napoleon's divisions at Jena in Saxony in 1806. Italy was stunned when its large army was overwhelmed by the Abyssinians at Adowa, in the arid plains of Ethiopia in 1896. Russia was trounced by Japan a decade later. It was unheard of that non-Europeans could inflict such damage upon "civilized" European powers.

In all those cases the initial emotions of consternation and grief were followed by earnest, often anguished debates about "what went wrong?" and "who is to blame?", and then by efforts to ensure that the debacles would never occur again. Coping with the injuries inflicted was replaced by policies of recovery, and not just in the armed forces. For example, the panoply of changes that was instituted in Britain following the Boer War ranged from such military matters as improved training, operations and intelligence to educational reforms, increases in business efficiency, and larger investments in technology. The Prussian nation's reforms were equally wide-ranging and purposeful. But Italy after the Adowa defeat was incapable of transforming itself, and Imperial Russia's loss to Japan was merely the harbinger of its external and internal collapse in 1917.

Such positive and negative examples are worth bearing in mind as the U.S. develops its own responses to the shock of September 11. It is clear that the terrorist attacks have led not just to short-term, military responses against the perpetrators but also to a re-examination of many aspects of the American way of life, of America's attitude toward other countries, and of the wellsprings of American power. In so many ways, the U.S. will have to think and act differently, and this transformation will have to be orchestrated from the top—president and Congress—testing our policy-making process to a degree not seen since 1941.

Moreover, because the U.S. has so many long-standing world interests to uphold in addition to the defeat of terrorism, it will have to establish priorities. For example, even as the U.S. Army takes on heightened responsibility for dealing with the Osama bin Ladens of this world, it will still have to defend South Korea against a large-scale infantry and tank attack from the North. By comparison, some American military commitments may have to be scaled back or reduced entirely, despite the inevitable complaints both at home and abroad. Intensified diplomatic and political efforts in Central Asia and the Persian Gulf will inevitably lead to less time being given to Latin America and Africa. To govern is to choose. And Great Powers are always engaged in balancing acts.

At the heart of this strategy lies the desire to ensure the long-term maintenance of American power in the troubled, unpredictable world of the early twenty-first century. At first sight, the foundations for sustaining that power position are impressive, perhaps deceptively so. Although the U.S. contains less than one-twentieth of the globe's population, it creates almost one-third of total world product. That is a

significant increase from a decade ago, due to Japanese stag-
nation and decline and Russian implosion, and an important
marker of America's long-term strength, assuming that that
share can be preserved.

More conspicuous still is U.S. military power. The world
has entered the twenty-first century with one country—
rather ironically, a republican democracy that suspects big
government—accounting for over one-third of all the
defense expenditures of all 190 countries on our planet. The
B-1 and B-52 bomber attacks upon the Taliban, the movement of carrier task forces into the Indian Ocean, the dis-
patch of Special Forces to Central Asia, the sophisticated
satellite-detection and electronic intelligence-gathering networks, suggest that the money was not misspent. But it is a
lot of money. The Pentagon's budget in the year 2000 was
equivalent to the combined defense spending of the next
nine largest military powers. There exists no equal in history
to such a disproportionate share, even if we went back to the
time of the Roman Empire.

Indeed, American strategic power is even greater than the
statistics suggest, since it is buttressed by an unrivalled technological and scientific base. A full 40 percent of all internet
traffic occurs in the U.S., and over 70 percent of all recent
Nobel laureates work in American universities and laboratories. Many of these world-class scientists not only conduct
experiments and make discoveries, they also teach future
scientists, thus replenishing one of the chief sources of
American strength and competitiveness.

In short, the U.S. has the material and military resources to maintain its power against any other state or even an alliance of states, provided those resources are wielded sensibly and are deployed against another nation in the traditional way. Indeed, if the present underpinnings of American national strength are not adequate for the destruction of enemy countries now, they will probably never be. Moreover, the U.S. is far more robust than Imperial Spain and late-Victorian Britain, which were faltering economically and technologically even as they were demonstrating their military and naval might in many theaters of war. Fifteen and twenty years ago the U.S. looked as if it, too, was faltering, but the collapse of the USSR, the weakening of Japan, and the remarkable recovery of American industrial competitiveness reversed those worrying trends, for a while at least. America's world position nowadays hardly looks in doubt.

But the problem with such a conclusion is that it assumes that the nature of power itself has not changed since Roosevelt and Churchill's time. Yet reflection on the meaning of bin Laden's attacks points to a more worrying thought, which is that today's threats may be much more difficult to handle precisely because force and power and threat have become much more diffuse. What was needed to defeat the Spanish Armada or Hitler's panzer columns may not be all that useful against a new amoeba-like foe, which attacks from within and through civilian instruments and in a decentralized and shadowy form. Creating an

American strategy to deal with this different form of enemy throws into doubt many of our existing assumptions and structures.

But even that recognition does not get to the central dilemma, which is that it will not be possible for the U.S. to pursue a Grand Strategy designed only to prevail in an age of terror. Rather, it will have to do that in conjunction with the maintenance of many of its traditional political and military goals, and in pursuit of objectives that have not disappeared simply because bin Laden arrived on our television screens. America may then need a hybrid strategy, a two-level policy, which is a strategist's nightmare because of the fear of crossed purposes and conflicting missions. And the U.S. government may be compelled repeatedly to change horses in mid-stream—to confront a terrorist threat on a Monday and a traditional type of threat in the Taiwan Straits on a Friday, or both together—which will make demands on our strategic judgment that would strain even Bismarck's genius.

To illustrate this point, let us look at the ways in which this hybrid strategic landscape—part terrorist, part traditional threat—will challenge the major elements of American Grand Strategy: that is, its military strength, its productive competitiveness, and its diplomatic skills. Each element is vital, and all three are under pressure.

I .

Of those components of present and future American power, the country's armed forces and military strength appear the easiest to maintain. Its defense-industrial base is far greater than that of any other power, or even of all of Europe combined. It possesses certain capabilities—global command and control systems, submarine-based nuclear missiles, long-range airlift, carrier task forces, "smart" weapons—that exist nowhere else and are probably too complex and expensive to be created by a rival state, at least in the next ten years. So long as the U.S. Congress is willing to give the Pentagon three hundred billion dollars or more each year in military expenditures, America should remain unchallenged by a single rising Great Power for a generation or more—just as Great Britain was unchallenged, in its naval and imperial spheres, after 1815. In the more distant future, say, the 2020s and 2030s, this may change in line with possible changes with the world's productive balances. But that is a matter of economic competitiveness, not of relative military might.

If there are weaknesses in America's present military stance they are likely to lie not in the grand totals of budgets and hardware, but in more subtle factors: in the transfusion of power, in the psychological realm, and, most dramatically, in the emergence of serious and sophisticated terrorism.

The first trend is the steady proliferation of home-based development of certain weapons systems in the rising states of Asia, especially China and India, and perhaps also Iran. The argument here is *not* that any of these nations will enter a direct and expensive head-to-head competition with the U.S. on the lines of, say, Admiral Tirpitz's creation of a German High Seas Fleet to challenge the Royal Navy in the years before 1914. Not only could these nations not afford it, but it simply isn't necessary for them to possess vast forces in order to create their own strategic "space" and push the American military presence a long way away from their own shores. With medium-range surface-to-ship and air-to-ship missiles, with their own nuclear warheads, and with a growing submarine fleet, they would increasingly make any American admiral nervous about bringing his aircraft carriers close to the Taiwan Strait or the Persian Gulf. It is, after all, the classical stratagem of the weaker power to develop weapons systems that exploit a chink in the superpower's armor, and it would be surprising if the rising Asian states did not follow such a course.

The second challenge is the unwillingness of the American democracy to accept high or even moderate military casualties, year after year, decade after decade. Much depends, of course, on the type of conflicts that the U.S. has to fight in the future. Ideally, the public would prefer to campaign in ways similar to the Gulf War of 1991 or the early stages of the fighting against the Taliban; that is, to conduct a war that is fought from afar, chiefly from the air and much less on the ground, with total control of the communications networks and with unbelievably light casualties on the

American side. This is an understandable desire, but is it realistic in a struggle against a nebulous and sometimes suicidal foe who resides in inhospitable terrain and is much less dependent upon modern infrastructure to sustain itself? No one doubts that the American public, convinced that it had to fight for its national survival, would be unrelenting in its pursuit of victory, as it was in 1941-1945. But would that American polity be so resolute if, year after year, it had to station troops in quasi-war/quasi-colonial-peacekeeping operations and receive news each week of a soldier lost here and a marine lost there to fanatics who were utterly careless of their own lives? Vietnam and Mogadishu still cast their shadows on the whole issue of ground deployments abroad.

Both of those challenges have been debated within the security studies community throughout the 1990s, leading to frequent calls for newer military doctrines—without, however, the armed services paying much apparent heed. But the third challenge to America's security and future, that of the skilled terrorism that occurred on September 11, brings demands of an entirely different order. The attackers were not distant Afrikaaner farmers, but sophisticated intruders using American instruments to inflict damage, and based in the U.S. itself. The coordination of the attacks was terrifying in its implications, and the symbolism of the buildings that were destroyed or damaged could not have been more obvious. Here was a weakness in our defenses created by one of our social strengths, namely, the permeability of American borders and the mobility and openness of America itself.

Indeed, this is so large a problem that even the expert panels and study groups that have called our attention to our vulnerabilities at home can only hint at the further awful possibilities. The Hart-Rudman Commission, which submitted its final report as late as March 2001, pointed gloomily and prophetically to a troubled future. Small and portable nuclear bombs, biological and chemical warfare, cyberterrorism, suicide-bombers on Amtrak or in synagogues, and even repeated false alarms about any of those dangers, can paralyze travel, damage the economy, sap confidence and spread fear. All are designed to penetrate and weaken the American and Western way of life, no matter how many supersonic fighter bombers we possess. All these dangers, in other words, are asymmetrical to our present defense structures.

Obviously, the Pentagon, State Department, NSC, indeed, the entire array of agencies that comprise America's national defense system are scrambling fast to reduce this asymmetry, as can be seen most dramatically in the creation, for the first time ever, of an Office of Homeland Security. This will be a task as long-lasting, as multilayered, and as demanding as the test that faced policymakers after 1945, when they had to put in place a totally different strategy for the altered strategic landscape that the unfolding cold war presented, and when they, too, could see no end to the newer type of struggle. Even so, there is a qualitative difference. America inherited or entered into many obligations in the decades after the Second World War, but all were subordinated to meeting the communist threat. Today, the U.S. simply does not have the luxury of concentrating all of its attention and resources on "beating the terrorists"; there are many other tasks for the world's Number One.

2.

The second, and equally important aspect of a strategy for sustaining America's position in the world over the long term is its continued economic growth, both in absolute terms and relative to others. Each of these caveats is vital. First, growth in absolute terms is a sine qua non. Despite the simplistic platforms of some American politicians for the "downsizing" of government, many trends in U.S. society point to the need for higher spending and perhaps a larger role for the state itself. The aging of the populace, the spiraling costs of health care and insurance, the need for massive investments in education, infrastructure and the environment, plus the panoply of calls to fund external aims—that is, defense, diplomacy, intelligence, foreign aid, international organizations—and the new costs for homeland security, are guaranteed to put enormous pressures upon the federal budget in the years to come. If the American economic pie stays the same size, or shrinks, it will be much harder to carry the newer fiscal burdens than if the gross domestic product steadily expands. An economy blighted by security concerns, a lack of confidence, reduced capital investment, and higher tax burdens is a worrisome prospect strategically.

Yet maintaining America's relative position economically is even more important than augmentations of wealth in absolute terms. There exist laissez-faire, free-market economists in this country today who proclaim that the more that the rest of the world embraces our way of life and achieves an equal standard of living, the better humankind will be. This may be true, in abstract, for humankind. But strategists and historians are likely to demur. Over time, broad changes in the relative productive capacity of nation-states do lead to changes in their relative power position. After all, the U.S. has been the supreme proof of that claim since at least a century ago. Had it not advanced from a cluster of scrimping, hard-won colonial outposts, to a broader-based agrarian and commercial land, to becoming the world's largest industrial producer, to its present status as the high-tech and financial superpower of our planet, it could not have redirected that economic muscle to its strategic and political purposes in crushing various enemies: Wilhelmine Germany, the Axis powers, Saddam Hussein. In December 1941, Imperial Japan made the mistake of attacking a nation with a GDP ten times its own size; this was tilting at windmills. The greater German Reich possessed about one-third of America's productive strength when it declared war upon the Republic a few days later. We may pay due tribute to the "band of brothers" memorializations of the Second World War and recognize individual acts of courage, but the old saying that a good big one will always beat a good little one still counts. It sounds crass to put it this way, but the U.S. won that war because in 1944, American factories built 94,000 planes and launched 30 aircraft carriers; and nobody else could compete.

From this hard-nosed strategic perspective, then, the accelerating forces of modernization and globalization which America is encouraging represent a double-edged sword, and to a degree that neither the policymakers in Washington nor the American public at large has properly appreciated until now. The assumption of the globalizers is that the interconnectedness of peoples and markets is inherently good. That is to say, the lowering of physical and fiscal barriers between countries, and the ever-increasing integration of their social activities each to another, are a benign and mutually satisfactory process, and therefore to be welcomed. If eighteenth-century Lancashire sends its textiles to Portugal, and Portugal sends its port wine to England, what could be nicer? And if twenty-first-century Arabia sends its petroleum to the U.S., and America exports its weapons to the Middle East, isn't that just fine?

There are, alas, a number of problems that confront this benign view of our planet's ever more integrated economic future. The first is that, the further one's economy moves away from a tight mercantilist model toward integration with the world economy, the more vulnerable it becomes to events outside its own control. The vulnerability could exist in a strictly military sense, such as dependence upon foreign petroleum supplies or upon non-U.S. producers of electronic chips for many of our weapons systems. But the vulnerability is there in a much broader sense, in that an open society can be hurt by attacks from clever and determined enemies, as was clearly seen on September 11. To have American civilian airliners hijacked and flown by pilots trained in the U.S. and launched in suicide attacks upon the World Trade Center was perhaps the ultimate example of an asymmetrical threat. As the country scrambles to learn lessons from those assaults, it faces the conundrum that has already tested the inhabitants of Tel Aviv, London, Belfast, Barcelona and elsewhere. No-one wants to reside in a totally closed society like North Korea, but complete integration and openness also bring their perils, and achieving a fine balance between accessibility *and* security will be excruciatingly difficult. Failing to find that successful balance will be extremely hurtful to America's economic future.

Another problem with the opening of all trade and fiscal barriers is that, economic activity seems to increase in general, it always seems to produce individual winners and losers—both countries and companies—and if there are too many of the latter, then social fabrics and political stability can be threatened. The Austrian economist Joseph Schumpeter's description of the "creative gales" of capitalism is useful here. The free-market system has proved better than any other in enhancing prosperity and supporting democracy, but a transition to the capitalist modes is often unsettling and sometimes risky. It has led to the collapse of older structures and ways of life, as well as to fresh opportunities. Many developing countries that have tried their best to embrace free-market policies—for example, in much of Latin America—have found this to be a rocky road to travel, with the goal of future prosperity by no means assured and great swaths of the public resentful and worried.

Since much of that hostile opinion regards the threat of modernization as being synonymous with Americanization rather than a broad global process, the U.S., its companies and its citizens are more likely to be blamed for the social and political costs of economic integration. When anti-U.S. riots have occurred in different parts of the world over the past years, it was not just the American flag that was attacked, but also symbols of American cultural and economic power such as McDonald's restaurants. Along with the attractiveness of American blue jeans and Marlboro Man and Coca-Cola to consumers worldwide go the disadvantages of being so visibly the symbols of change and challenge to societies not equipped to respond smoothly to the free-market message, or opposed to social and cultural transformation.

Finally, there is the age-old test of how the number one economy goes about maintaining its relative advantage vis-à-vis other nations, decade after decade, when it is simultaneously calling upon the rest of the planet to imitate and emulate its methods and successes. As noted above, this has never seemed a problem to the free-market proponents of the "borderless world," since in their view the rising tide of global prosperity lifts all boats and there is no reason to

resent others catching up. Besides, they argue, since traditional national economies are becoming less and less
important players as compared to giant multinational corporations, it is anachronistic to worry about the relative
position of states.

Such an attitude cannot be shared by strategists studying
national and international power; for them it is precisely the
relative distribution of strength and influence that is at the
core of understanding world politics and the whole dynamic
of "the rise and fall of the Great Powers" over the centuries.
For the U.S. to lose its share of global productive power and
prosperity in the years to come would be the same as Spain's
losing ground to the Dutch republic in the seventeenth century, or the overtaking of Britain's position by both Germany
and America early in the twentieth century. The president
and the U.S. Congress are clearly aware of the unwelcome
consequences that would flow from a long-term relative
decline on the economic front; even the impressive growth
spurt of the 1990s has not erased the seriousness of the
"decline" debate that captured attention in the previous
decade. In fact, many of the lessons learned from that recovery—reducing the national debt and freeing up more capital
for investment, trimming taxes, encouraging business to
restructure itself and to move into new markets and products—are a hopeful indicator of how to stay competitive. But
whether the process of economic and technological renewal
can be carried out successfully, again and again, is impossible
to predict. No country has managed it forever.

There is a deeper contradiction in America's eagerness to spread its economic recipes for success to all the world, which may be summed up in the following question: "What if all the world *is* raised up to the level of Kansas?" What if the American level of prosperity was reached in many of the less developed states of today? The results—assuming a global environmental collapse could be avoided during that burst of economic activity—would be beneficial to billions of people, but not to American relative power. A mere glance at the statistics concerning, say, America and China tells us why. As noted above, the U.S. presently contains around 4.6 percent of the world's population, whereas China possesses about 21 percent. But the former is a stronger power than the latter because its gross domestic product per capita is $34,200 per annum whereas China's is a mere $3,900. However, should the time come when China's people have the same average standard of living as that enjoyed by Americans, its absolute economic heft would be four to five times larger—a fact few people in this country would relish. For years now, China's economy has been growing at least twice as fast as America's, if not even faster, and the more that the U.S. invests in that country, encourages its membership in the World Trade Organization and supports international credits to China, the narrower becomes the economic gap between the two nations.

That gap is still large, people might reply, but one cannot help being reminded of the way in which Great Britain's outpourings of capital, machinery and factories, and new productive techniques led to the industrialization of

Germany and the U.S. in the late nineteenth century and to their reduction and then elimination of Britain's early lead. This is not the only historical example of where the front-runner helped to create its own successors. Yet no one in Washington argues that it might be imprudent, strategically, to assist China's long-term growth, and that where things stand now is perfectly satisfactory; on the contrary, many do argue that the greater the prosperity and commercial openness that China achieves can only be good for America. Perhaps this optimism rests upon the unspoken assumption will become a stable, peaceful democracy, and that America has nothing to fear. But the overtaking of Britain by the U.S. a century ago also involved two democracies, and the declining country found the process a painful one.

It will be countered that the process of globalization is so widespread and pervasive that there really is no alternative to it, since no sensible person wishes to see a return to the autarkic and protectionist policies of the 1930s. This is probably true. The internet is here to stay, financial controls would be difficult to reimpose, round-the-clock trading is a reality. The genie is out of the bottle and putting it back in would probably break the glass. But even if the U.S. cannot control the tides of change, it is curious that the rosy assumptions about the economic transformation of our planet are not more keenly scrutinized.

3.

The third and final component of a long-term American strategy for the maintenance of its power and influence lies in the realm of diplomacy—in its application of diplomatic skills, in its empowerment and utilization of international organizations, in its clever alliance-building, in its shrewd intelligence-gathering and sharing. These were not strong features of the present administration's policies during its first eight months, but the shock of September 11 also caused the disappearance of American unilateralism, and at many levels. The uses of the United Nations Organization—ranging from the early warning of crises, to food distribution to refugees, to Security Council authorizations, to the challenge of nation-building after wars—are now better appreciated. All of them will be needed to augment U.S. purposes, as will the panoply of assistance that can be provided by the World Bank and the International Monetary Fund, by Interpol and by foreign and international criminal-justice institutions. The very nature of the international terrorist threat, and the delicacy of U.S. relations with the Muslim world, place a premium upon smart diplomacy.

But this in turn could involve significant trade-offs, over which the U.S. may have little choice. Countries like India and Brazil, Germany and Japan, which for years have pushed for a reexamination of the United Nations' governing structures, especially the Security Council, may want to leverage

America's new appreciation of international forums and programs to ask for changes. And "veto powers" like China and Russia will probably also want to see U.S. concessions, both positive and negative, in return for their longer-lasting support of American actions. Empowering the international financial and development agencies with fresh resources to deal with the challenges of widespread poverty, malnutrition and human rights abuses will require America to step right up to the table, but as primus inter pares and not as the unchallenged boss, and with more money than it has been prepared to spend recently for such causes.

Moreover, the war against terrorism will place even greater demands than before upon the diplomacy of relating to unsavory regimes. This is of course not the first time that the American democracy has had strange bedfellows; the exigencies of the cold war caused the U.S. to give aid to dictatorships and right-wing military groups in different parts of the world, and to compromise human rights standards. This is always difficult for an open and opinionated democracy, especially when the Constitution gives the Congress such a large role in foreign policymaking. Now, the identification of terrorist networks as America's greatest foe, and the embrace of any government that helps to crush terrorism, could prove a dubious and counter-productive litmus test for long-term diplomacy. Large powers who maltreat their ethnic and religious minorities—Russia in Chechnya, China in Tibet and Xinjiang—may be pardoned, or at least their actions ignored. Countries that were regarded with dislike and suspicion—

one thinks of the murderous regime in the Sudan—may now be rewarded if they come out against international terrorism, as if their suppressions were not another form of terrorism. Shaky conservative governments in the Middle East that are not democracies and that fear their own people may be supported. All alliances, the British historian Lord Beloff once wrote, "involve servitudes." America seems willing at present to run that risk, but the old Arab saying that the enemy of my enemy is my friend also seems fraught with danger. The moral philosopher's teaching about the "unintended consequences" of a certain act will be witnessed again and again. In sum, the years ahead will bring testing times for the State Department and the U.S. Foreign Service, even if it also brings them more resources and respect.

Finally, there is the danger of overreaction and overextension. The U.S. has received a dreadful and unjustified shock, and is reacting to that blow with a combination of policies, all aimed at punishing terrorists and their supporters and, more broadly, maintaining its interests and its position in a deeply troubled world. Amidst this grief and shock, it is no surprise to hear angry voices call for the return of some form of Western colonialism—this time, apparently benign—for the reinvention of "mandates" in the Middle East, for a large-scale military presence in Afghanistan and neighboring states. All of this threatens to take American troops further and further away from their own country, though presumably in the cause of "homeland security."

Such calls for the insertion of a long-term American presence somewhere in the middle of the Hindu Kush deserve skepticism and caution, however well intentioned they may be. If we have learned anything from the 20th century, it must be John Stuart Mill's warning that "such a thing as the government of one people by another does not and cannot exist." Punishing raids against terrorist bases and brutal regimes are one thing. Imperial policing by the American democracy is something else, politically divisive and ultimately debilitating, and thus counter to a reasoned strategy for the maintenance of American power in the twenty-first century.

This raises, then, the ultimate political question, and an insidious one: is the very striving for the maintenance of America's present place in the world actually desirable? Throughout this essay the assumption has been that preserving the position of "America as Number One" was the only Grand Strategy conceivable, and that all that was at issue was whether our policies were wise enough to achieve that goal in an age where new threats mingled with old. But what if a younger generation of Americans in, say, the 2020s or 2030s comes to a different conclusion? What if they favor the diffusion of power and responsibility and burden, and a voluntary alteration of America's role from being the hegemonic policeman to being the senior partner in a world of democratic states that work out global problems through international structures and shared policies? This sounds fanciful in our present age of terror and war, poverty and hatreds. But the human imagination is occasionally permitted to envision a future for this planet in which real democratic representation, from local government to world bodies, exists; human rights are universally respected; a more equitable prosperity is enjoyed; and the "world community" really is that. To get there, however, would involve far greater strategic rethinking than is being forced upon us by the existing crisis.

Furthermore, even those Americans hostile to the very notion of the sharing of global power and of the U.S. becoming a "normal" country may sooner or later have to accept that it is unavoidable, and is in fact going to happen because of the very sort of liberal nation and open society that we are. The terrorist threat, committed within our own borders though planned from thousands of miles away, has shown that we need the rest of the world and cannot ignore it. We cannot avoid making diplomatic compromises, and we can no longer shun or scorn international organizations. Above all, we cannot stop long-term shifts in the economic and strategic balances, because by our economic and social policies we ourselves are the very artificers of those future changes; we can no more stop the rise of Asia than we can stop the winter snows and the summer heat. Whether we accept that transformation gracefully and manage the relative change in America's world position with adroitness—or, instead, resent and combat that secular trend, insisting that the U.S. is exceptional—may be the biggest strategic question of all.

For the present, however, it seems that there are resources enough—military, economic, technological, diplomatic, intellectual—for the preservation of the U.S.'s place in the world, albeit perhaps in a more chastened, thoughtful and careful mode. The challenge is to use those resources wisely, for wisdom is the bedrock upon which successful policy rests. But this test of our wisdom will be greater than it was before September 11 because the terrorist attacks changed the meaning of power—not entirely, but to a degree that forces us to re-examine so much of America's policies and assumptions. Caught between a familiar and imposing agenda of international security concerns, and a new, unfamiliar and equally daunting agenda of the struggle against terrorism, the U.S. ship of state may find the waters through which it passes in the twenty-first century even more tricky to navigate, and even more turbulent, than those of the century just gone.

CHAPTER 4

A HERCULEAN TASK: THE MYTH AND REALITY OF ARAB TERRORISM

Charles Hill

TERRORISM THRIVES ON myth. So does the on-going struggle against terrorism. Four deceptive and dangerous delusions have been in the air since September 11. One is that America faces an entirely new kind of challenge—that nothing of this sort has happened before, that our life as a people will be changed forever. Then there is the myth that we brought this on ourselves: if only we had not been so arrogant, if only we had listened and learned from others, if only we had conducted our foreign policy differently, this catastrophe could have been forestalled. What the U.S. could and should have done over the past decade was to act more swiftly and decisively against terrorism. There is also the myth that "one man's terrorist is another man's freedom fighter," that legitimate grievances about poverty and oppression leave those afflicted with no choice but to take up terrorism. Finally, there is the lament that nothing we do can be

effective against such a threat; that our enemy thrives in shadowy corners of the world and contrives schemes that are
beyond the reach of our intelligence capabilities and military
might.

The beginning of wisdom is dispelling the myths and
looking reality in the eye.

I.

The war against terrorism that began on September 11,
2001, is the second such campaign that the U.S. has waged.
The first began in the 1970s and continued through most
of the 80s. Many have forgotten that we even fought that
war—and that we won. It's worth remembering now that
commercial aircraft and cruise ships were seized by specialists in murder. Innocent civilians died in Munich, London,
Paris, Istanbul and Delhi. Assassins struck down Anwar
Sadat, the president of Egypt, four years after his historic
visit to Jerusalem in search of peace with Israel. For
Americans that first war against terrorism was marked by a
long series of assaults, hostage-takings, and murders. Our
ambassador to Sudan was murdered by Palestinians in 1973;
our ambassador to Lebanon was murdered in 1976; our citizens were taken hostage from the American embassy in
Tehran in 1979; that same year the American ambassador in
Kabul, Afghanistan was kidnapped and murdered; TWA
Flight 843 was hijacked to Beirut in 1983, and an American

citizen, Leon Klinghoffer, was murdered by terrorists who pushed him in his wheelchair into the sea after they seized the Mediterranean cruise ship *Achille Lauro*.

Then, that same year, the American embassy in Beirut was blown up by a car bomb that killed 46 people, including 16 Americans. Six months later terrorists drove a van packed with explosives into the U.S. Marines barracks compound at Beirut airport, killing 241 men. When President Reagan linked the bombing of a Berlin discotheque in 1985 to Libya's leader, Muammar Qaddafi, the president ordered U.S. Air Force F-111s to bomb Libyan installations and Qaddafi's own compound in April 1986; Qaddafi escaped but one of his daughters was reported killed. Following the raid, Qaddafi's willingness to use terror against Americans seemed to fade. By the end of the 1980s, it appeared that the primary figures in the terrorist world were largely suppressed or on the run.

The terrorists in this first war were driven primarily by political motives. The Palestine Liberation Organization's actions were aimed at destroying "the Zionist Entity"— Israel—and establishing a secular, social democratic, multi-religious state. The Popular Front for the Liberation of Palestine—a constant source of terrorist activity against Israeli targets—has always been an explicitly secular organization. The main state supporters of terrorism in the first war, Syria and Iraq, were founded on the pan-Arab al-Ba'th movement—ostensibly socialist but actually fascist—and their leaders were known for their ruthless suppression of radical Islamist challengers.

In retrospect, one attack on Americans during that first war anticipated the religious element in the terrorism that we're seeing during the second one. In November 1979, Islamist radicals seized and held the Grand Mosque in Mecca until Saudi Arabian forces captured and killed them. This shocking event was an entirely Muslim affair, but in reaction, religious radicals in Pakistan rioted against the U.S. and set fire to the American embassy in Islamabad, a vivid example of the widespread suspicion that a sinister American hand is at work in virtually every occurrence in the Middle East.

2.

The first war against terrorism was left unfinished and unwon. Qaddafi, it turned out, had by no means abandoned terrorism. In hindsight, he emerges as a transitional figure between the first and second terrorist wars. After Qaddafi took power in 1969, he decreed that the Libyan flag would be changed to solid, unadorned green, a statement that no regime could be more Islamic than his. He openly proclaimed that he was locked in a religious conflict with the West. President Reagan's air strikes against Qaddafi, which the U.S. considered successful at the time, turned out to have been a superficial and unsustained gesture. The Americans could hit hard, but they didn't carry through effectively. Qaddafi simply lowered his profile and planned, along with other Middle Eastern state supporters of terrorism, the destruction in 1989 of Pan Am Flight 103 over Scotland by a bomb planted on board. The U.S. had not yet learned that retaliation only generates another round of terrorism; eradication is the only way to get rid of the threat.

The inadequacies of U.S. antiterrorist policy only worsened when the U.S. decided to pursue those responsible for the bombing of Pan Am 103 through international legal means and, later, through the efforts of the United Nations secretary-general. Throughout the 1990s the U.S. relied heavily on law enforcement mechanisms to try to investigate and punish terrorists. The results, predictably, were interminable legalistic entanglements that focused on the lowest suspects and left the masterminds alone. Courtroom standards of evidence served the interests of international terrorist networks and the states that supported them.

Following each major terrorist attack on U.S. targets in the past five years—the huge bomb that killed nineteen American military personnel and wounded hundreds in the Khobar Towers hotel in Saudi Arabia on June 25, 1996; the bombing of the American embassies in Kenya and Tanzania on August 7, 1998; the attack on the USS *Cole* in Yemen on October 12, 2000—President Clinton vowed that those responsible would be brought to justice. In no case was effective U.S. action taken. After a news cycle or two had passed, media attention dwindled and the terrorist attacks faded from the public's consciousness.

The U.S. pattern of reaction was to act quickly but without a sustained effort. Launching cruise missiles might be portrayed as a bold and decisive move, even though the missiles seemed designed to inflict minimal harm. This pattern was capped in 1998, when the U.S. ceased to make any effective sanction efforts against Saddam Hussein. As a result, the Iraqi dictator, who was left in place by the U.S. after the end of the Gulf War in 1991, was allowed to go from strength to strength in the decade since then. Today he has reestablished himself as a formidable presence in the Middle East and as the owner of an increasing array of weapons of mass destruction.

3.

Two professional fields of endeavor have contributed to this pattern of U.S. behavior: journalism and diplomacy—the media and the mediators. Paradoxically, the greater the U.S. involvement in a globalizing world became, the less knowledgeable or concerned Americans became about events beyond their own borders. The media turned inward, along with the White House, closing overseas bureaus, replacing foreign affairs coverage with personal lifestyle features, growing less interested and less informed year by year, coming alive only when the possibility arose that American servicemen and -women might come home in body bags. The media failed to report when U.S. foreign policymakers set deadlines but failed to enforce them, made threats but never carried them out, blamed others—such as the United

Nations—for American failures, and altered long-established principles for some marginal advantage in domestic politics, steadily losing credibility with both allies and adversaries.

The deterioration in the quality and attention span of press coverage found a parallel in American diplomacy. Throughout the 1990s, slipshod, quick-fix negotiations were aimed at getting an agreement, almost any agreement, and working out the details later. The diplomatic interventions of former president Carter responded to the "needs" of dictators in North Korea, Bosnian Serbia, and Haiti. Today's diplomatic success became tomorrow's dangerous morass. The heralded Dayton Accords of 1995 created two real but diplomatically nonrecognized states—a Muslim-Croatian "confederation" and a Bosnian "Serb republic"—supposedly under an internationally recognized but politically unreal Federation of Bosnia-Herzegovina. Subsequent agreements and understandings regarding Kosovo and Macedonia became, each in its own way, variations on this impossible theme.

The 1998 "Good Friday" agreement in Northern Ireland followed a diplomatic fad with the bizarre label "consociationalism"—that is, everyone takes part in everything with everyone else: north-south arrangements to please those who want Ulster united with Ireland, and east-west measures for those who want it to be forever tied to Britain. The fatal flaw in the text was its studied avoidance of the Irish Republican Army's determination to keep its arsenal of weapons. The Irish agreement still beguiles hopeful observers but must be put down as a failure.

Add the string of professionally negotiated but loophole-riddled treaty drafts on climate change, nuclear testing, and an international criminal court, and a decade-long record of diplomatic malpractice emerges. The belief has taken hold that any agreement is better than no agreement, and that once an agreement has been reached, peace is primarily a matter of good administration.

4.

The most frequent charge that the U.S. has fallen short in the past and now must change its ways features Israel and the American role in negotiations between Palestinians and Israelis. Assertions that the U.S. must become more "even-handed" are grossly misplaced.

Over the years, we have seen that whenever Israelis and Palestinians have come close to a peace agreement, the terrorists have stepped up their attacks. They abhor the idea of such a peace.

The Arab-Israeli peace process has been based on the acceptance of United Nations Security Council Resolution No. 242, passed in 1967 in the wake of the Six-Day War that Egypt, Syria, Jordan and Iraq waged against Israel. The underlying idea of Resolution 242 was that negotiations between the two sides would eventually lead to an exchange of territory for peace, with Israel ceding the West Bank and Gaza and the Palestinians recognizing Israel's legitimate existence as a state.

At the Clinton–Barak–Arafat meeting at Camp David in the summer of 2000, the Israeli prime minister offered what amounted to giving up the last of Israel's once nonnegotiable "red lines," including Palestinian statehood and a Palestinian governmental presence in Jerusalem. But the chairman of the Palestinian Authority, Yasser Arafat, would respond to nothing Israel proposed.

Thus, the logic of a negotiated peace process was shattered. Within weeks Arafat launched an *intifada*, a Palestinian uprising with terrorist operations at its core. Israel no longer had an Arab negotiating partner willing to talk seriously about peace.

Arab terrorism, with its commitment to the eradication of Israel, is the principal cause of the collapse of the peace process. A diabolical logic chain has formed: terrorism's primary targets are virtually all of the Middle Eastern regimes— not just Israel's but those of the surrounding Arab countries as well. Fear of being overthrown by terrorists leads those regimes to inundate their people with anti-Israel propaganda in order to divert them toward external targets. Israel's willingness in recent years to abandon its formerly nonnegotiable positions and the withdrawal of Israel Defence Forces from southern Lebanon and offer to give up the Golan Heights to Syria has only created a conviction among Arabs that terrorism is working and that no accommodation of Israel in any form need be considered.

Indeed, were peace between Israel and Palestine to be agreed to in this context, the regimes of the Middle East would panic in fear that the terrorists they have harbored would turn on them.

Thus the terrorists, the regimes that foster yet fear them, and most recently the Palestinian leadership, all now share one big idea: none at present can tolerate a peace agreement between Israelis and Palestinians.

Those who think that the U.S. can defuse Islamic fundamentalist rage and end terrorism by imposing a peace agreement are out of touch with the cruel reality of the Middle East. To press now for such a peace is to invite further terror. Anyone who has been seriously involved in the diplomacy of the Arab-Israeli conflict over the years, as I have been, understands that peace cannot be imposed, under duress, from the outside. To attempt such a solution would shield one side or the other, or both, from the need to make the concessions necessary for a durable agreement. Under present circumstances, any indication that the U.S. is considering a dictated peace will be taken by the Arab side as an immense victory and a way station on the road to totally eliminating the State of Israel.

It is clear that only after Islamic terrorism is eradicated can an Israeli-Palestinian peace agreement be achieved. Only after the American war on terrorism is won can peace in the Middle East become possible. The same holds true for many other supposedly intractable conflicts around the world; it is the terrorists who reject the very idea of peace. Suppress terrorism and diplomacy will get a new lease on life.

In the aftermath of the September 11 mass murders, many
Americans admirably rushed to recommit themselves to civil
liberties and respect for the rights of individuals who share
the appearance, ethnicity, or faith of the terrorist enemies of
the U.S. The religious dimension of this terrorism, however,
cannot be explained away. This version of Islam undeniably
involves religious leaders instructing their followers that it is
their religious duty to kill those who do not share their religious belief. Islam justifiably can be considered a faith that
has fostered peace and civilization. But like some other religions, Islam has, during certain periods of history and in certain parts of the globe, been part of an environment where
evildoers can burrow and breed. The higher levels of Islam
have not yet displayed adequate doctrinal defenses against
this, nor have they credibly condemned it. There has been a
deafening silence from the clerical hierarchy in most countries, including those considered to be moderate. The Friday
sermons in mosques across the Middle East, and in Europe
and North America as well, have ranged from a pro–Taliban
line to a transparent apologia for the terrorists at best; i.e.
what they did was bad but understandable and no worse than
the "terrorism" conducted by the U.S. and Israel.

Much public argumentation in the aftermath of the
September 11 attacks has sidestepped this reality by stressing
the anger and desperation that must be felt by those peoples
of the Middle East who lead lives of poverty, unemployment,
and dispossession.

But the terrorists we pursue today are not the poor and downtrodden. In case after case we see that they come from strong families, well-off and educated, literate and with perfectly realistic prospects for their lives and careers ahead. Most notably, Mohammed Atta, who flew American Airlines Flight 11 into the North Tower of the World Trade Center, was the well-educated, well-traveled son of an affluent Cairo attorney.

Something else is at work here, something other than the idea that the angry poor turn terrorist. That "something else" is frustration over the region's humiliating failure to succeed economically and resentment at the absence of political avenues toward progress.

Not many years ago, the states of the Arab Middle East seemed well placed to join Asian nations as entrants to the "First World." In geographic extent, population size, and wealth, the region was an obvious candidate for world power and influence. Even without substantial oil resources, the Middle East and North Africa should command geopolitical importance by the shape and location of their lands on the globe.

But the Arab-Islamic world has not attained full participation in the global economy. As the renowned Princeton historian Bernard Lewis noted over a decade ago, "The question is being asked in a new and more relevant, and therefore more painful form. Why has the Islamic world not been able to parallel the economic and political modernization of . . . other non-Western civilizations?"

Some economists of the Muslim world have argued that the Koran points toward the economic policy that Islamic communities should adopt: a capitalist one based on market forces. And *The Economist* has noted that "Islamic banking is not merely consistent with capitalism (ie, with a market-driven allocation of capital, labour and other resources) but in certain respects may be better suited to it than western banking." In Koranic theory, at least, an economic reward should become available for distribution only if consumption forgone is translated into investment that yields a real economic return. Lenders are entitled to part of any such return, according to Islam, but only to the extent that they help to create wealth.

Thus all the legal and institutional prerequisites for financing and administering "capitalist" production and exchange, and all the skills of calculation of comparative costs and advantages in various fields of investment, were in place in the Islamic world long before Europeans employed them effectively in the modern era.

Nothing in the Koran seems to inhibit a thriving commerce. Muhammad was a businessman in origin, and Mecca was an important center for commerce. The Koran contains specific portions on the practice of business. Just as the rise of modern capitalism in Europe was accompanied by a new religious attitude toward making money, so the bourgeois revolution of the Muslim Empire of the eighth and ninth centuries had a strong religious foundation.

Arabs were at the heart of a vast world trading system during the empire of the Abbasid caliphs, who ruled from

Baghdad for two hundred years starting in the middle of the eighth century. They created a rich and sprawling consumer market. Abbasid silver poured into Russia and Scandinavia for timber, to the African coast for slaves, to Canton for ceramics. Before civil war and heedless overspending exhausted this economy, Baghdad was the center of a global economy spanning an incredible array of differing peoples. As a soldier-scholar of the British Empire, Sir John Bagot Glubb wrote, "Under Caliph Haroun al-Rashid, who ruled from the late eighth century into the early ninth, the empire achieved its high noon of glory and wealth, comparable perhaps to Victorian England. . . . Arab merchants did business in China, Indonesia, India and East Africa. Their ships were by far the largest and the best appointed in Chinese waters or in the Indian Ocean. Under their highly developed banking system, an Arab businessman could cash a check in Canton on his bank account in Baghdad." It was a great era of science and culture as well: mathematics, medicine, astronomy, poetry, and philosophy, with the words of Aristotle, Plato, Hippocrates, and Galen translated into Arabic. Haroun al-Rashid was a patron of philosophy, medicine, mathematics and poetry and his rule was rich in works of science, scholarship and the arts.

As the American journalists who lodged and watered at the al-Rashid Hotel in Baghdad in 1990-1991 during Desert Storm were made aware, that age of glory remains vivid in the contemporary Arab-Islamic mind. The partial fulfillment, yet ultimate frustration, of seemingly limitless political and economic possibilities has left in Islam a residue of poignant but highly volatile memories, which ceaselessly influence attitudes in contemporary Muslim politics.

Some Islamic governments have explored ways to do, in effect, what European and English Puritanism is said to have done for capitalism: harness the disciplines of fundamentalist religious doctrine with the highest form of economic efficiency. An international conference in Mecca in 1976 led to the establishment at Saudi Arabia's King Abdulaziz University of a Center for Research in Islamic Economics. Visitors to the center, such as I, learn that its mission is to "structure and spread an awareness of economic thought and considerations based on Islamic principles." There seems no obstacle based in economics to the successful accomplishment of that mission.

For most of the past quarter century, the Arab world appeared to be one of the foremost financial powers in the world. In the 1970s, the industrial nations of the West seemed trapped by their reliance on oil. As revenues for the Gulf countries and Libya reached unprecedented levels, there seemed to be no limit to Arab oil power. OPEC set prices as high as $40 a barrel for crude that cost less than 50 cents to produce. The bold and deft strokes that brought Gulf and peninsular oil resources under control of an Arab cartel displayed world-class political talents.

But the terms of trade have followed a generally unfavorable course for oil producers. Oil revenues declined from their peak in 1980 (from about $225 billion per year to about

$55 billion at present). Oil revenues go to the producer-country regime, reinforcing their views of themselves as dispensers of bounty. A rapidly growing population expects a level of benefits from government that cannot be sustained over time owing to government's declining revenues and failure to diversity its economy and range of exports. The possession of oil resources creates an expectation of widespread prosperity while deterring the regimes from taking serious measures to build a healthy, broad-based economy. Were it not for oil, the Middle East would rank lower than Africa in economic development.

Middle Eastern regimes base their power on a form of compact with the people that economic and social realities make virtually impossible to fulfill. As discontent grows, the tenets of an ever more fundamentalist religion provide grounds for an attack on any government in power, whatever its form or philosophy.

5.

If neither history nor the authentic Islamic faith can account for the Middle East's lowly world ranking, what can? The answer lies in the miserable state of politics and governance in that region.

States are the building blocks and fundamental actors of international relations, and diplomacy is the method by which states address and attempt to solve problems that arise among them. The Islamic political tradition, however, stresses a seamless unity of faith and power, a concept that can be portrayed as incompatible with the very idea of statehood.

Traditional Islamic governance is based on the *umma*, the community of believers, which should know no boundaries other than the religion itself. *Sharia*—law based on a literal reading of the Koran—takes priority over the state and, indeed, does not require the existence of a state. The Caliphate emerged from the need, following the Prophet's death, to establish a politico-religious center of power. In the modern era the Ottoman Empire claimed the Caliphate. In 1924, when the Turkish revolution overthrew the Ottomans, the Caliphate was abolished.

Since then, Arab-Islamic political elites have failed to find a credible alternative to the traditional system of government. At present, the shadow of illegitimacy falls over all political power in Islam, and the very existence of states may be seen as evidence of non-Islamic practices. This grim reality makes all the more potent the seemingly fantastical suggestions that some charismatic figure like Osama bin Laden could, through terrorist warfare, cleanse the Dar al Islam, the realm of Islam, of all unbelievers and reestablish the Caliphate.

The Arab world today consists of twenty-one countries that are members of the League of Arab States, few of which seem comfortable with their own statehood except as a means of providing a veil of international legitimacy to their own version of power politics. Some, like Morocco, are hereditary paternalistic monarchies whose royal heads are uneasy indeed. Some are secular regimes on the national socialist model, dominated by the Ba'th party, whose boundaries, like Iraq's, originated in the age of European colonialism. Still others, like Egypt and Syria, borrowed Western constitutional forms that never have achieved legitimacy because they have not been accompanied by democratic freedoms. A look at the region as a whole reveals inauthentic "states" attempting to function within the concept of pan-Arabism ("There is only one Arab nation") within the wider body of states with a commitment to pan-Islam, members of the Organization of the Islamic Conference, where, if anywhere, the unfilled office of the Caliphate resides. All these concepts hamper the full participation of the region in the contemporary international system of states. The absence of credible political systems, and their inability to hold their own in a world of state powers, incites peoples to protest under the banner of Islam.

Over the past decade, an immense contradiction has become ever more evident between the ideals of pan-Arabism and pan-Islam on the one hand and efforts at state-strengthening on the other. State security has been tightened, as has state control over the media. Legitimate opposition elements have been crushed, bought off, or co-opted.

As the regimes try to ride these two horses, what on the surface appears to be a variety of governmental forms begins to emerge as variations of a single approach to the political ordering of society. In Oman, a sultan; in Yemen, a military "president"; in Saudi Arabia, a king and family with special Islamic custodial responsibilities; in Jordan, a king of a simulated constitutional monarchy; in Egypt, a president and a parliament only nominally connected to the original Western meaning of those institutions. Beneath all these styles a single form is discernible. Power is held by a strongman, surrounded by a praetorian guard.

A family or personal entourage clusters around and profits from the ruler's position. Those close to power gain; the weak are disregarded. There is a constant fear that repressed opposition will attempt a coup d'état. This pattern represents the most fundamental and ancient political order.

6.

The country in the Arab–Islamic world that most vividly embodies these contradictions is Saudi Arabia. It is no accident that this fragile, impacted, conflict-ridden country should be not just the homeland of Osama bin Laden but also the source of his fortune.

The only nation-state with a family name and the only state whose legitimacy is based on its protection of Islam, Saudi Arabia is considered by its monarchy to be a complete embodiment of Islam through the kingdom's strict application of *Sharia*. Indeed, with its vast oil wealth, huge expenditures on infrastructure and private enterprise, and enthusiasm for expanding science and higher education, Saudi Arabia can be viewed as a great experiment to determine whether modern economic and technological life can be achieved in compatibility with the most rigorous interpretation of Islam regarding such matters as separation of the sexes and adherence to practices that depart significantly from an emerging global consensus on human rights and procedural justice.

Saudi Arabia's rulers focus on three areas of concern: preservation of the monarchy and rule by the immense body of princes of the house (no constitution, no political parties, no elections); preserving a stable and long-term market for its oil—and a healthy Western economy dependent upon it (e.g., strongly opposing carbon-emission taxes in the West); and protecting Saudi financial assets and, perhaps most fundamental, its legitimacy and reputation as "custodian" of the two holy mosques of Islam at Mecca and Medina, sites for the pilgrimage required of all the world's Muslims. The regime goes to great lengths to avoid contact between its population and the non-Islamic world, not an easy task when 4 million of the country's 11 million population are expatriates whose labor is necessary to carry forward the ambitious modernization policies of the rulers. Tourism is actively opposed for this same reason.

Yet Saudi Arabia, for all its intense application of the Koran to every aspect of society, is denounced as virtually non-Islamic by the new wave of terrorists. In 1996 bin Laden issued a fatwa, a religious decree on a matter of Islamic law, setting as his primary goals the takeover of Mecca and Medina and the overthrow of the Saudi regime. This cannot be achieved, bin Laden's pronouncements make clear, as long as the U.S. has any presence or influence in the Islamic world.

Every regime of the Arab-Islamic world has proved a failure. Not one has proved able to provide its people with realistic hope for a free and prosperous future. The regimes have found no way to respond to their people's frustration other than a combination of internal oppression and propaganda to generate rage against external enemies. Religiously inflamed terrorists take root in such soil. Their threats to the regimes extort facilities and subsidies that increase their strength and influence. The result is a downward spiral of failure, fear, and hatred.

Such feelings are deepened by a cultural infection that has spread all across the Middle East: the deeply rooted conviction that virtually every significant occurrence is caused by some external conspiracy. Every societal shortcoming is attributed to a foreign plot, and every local problem is believed to be beyond solution without some decision—perniciously withheld—made in the U.S. or some other foreign power center.

Over the past few decades, Americans have begun to fall prey to an inverse version of the conspiracy-theory mentality: that virtually every problem in the world can be attributed to some fault of ours.

Conspiracy theories blight every society they touch. The people who hold them become impervious to evidence and reason. The bizarre interaction between the Middle Eastern and American strains of this disease is becoming highly deleterious.

7.

Nevertheless, the situation in the Middle East presents some opportunities to shape the region and the international scene in a positive way. Many governments of the Arab-Islamic region who have accommodated terrorists and provided support for them have felt a shock of recognition at the September 11 attacks on the U.S. These regimes have been playing a dangerous game, stirring up their people's hatred of external forces but trying not to let the balance of power shift to the terrorists themselves. The attacks on New York City and Washington, D.C., made clear that the beast is on the loose and may escape the control of its keepers.

The success of Arab-Islamic terrorism has been emulated by violent disaffected groups in every part of the world. And governments in regions other than the Middle East have tried their own forms of appeasement. European countries in particular have taken a benign view of the presence of foreign terrorist organizations in their cities in a kind of tacit agreement that "we won't bother you if you don't target us." Throughout much of the first war on terrorism, for example, Vienna provided a comfortable home base for numerous terrorists. The deal worked well for Austria, which was virtually immune from terrorist attacks for years. Now all nations need to recognize that these deals are too dangerous—to the world economy and every nation's stake in it, if nothing else—to be allowed in the future.

Above all the U.S. needs to restore its credibility as an international presence for stability and security. While America has become an omnipresent cultural and commercial force, its staying power when it comes to helping protect others from the world's human predators has not been impressive in recent years. It will not be easy to regain the stature that we once had. As in the classic American western *High Noon*, the courageous sheriff finds no support when the villain comes back to town, because the townspeople's fear of danger to themselves from the showdown, coming closer with every tick of the clock, outweighs their willingness to fight to restore law and order to their town. The last time that the U.S. visibly and definitively displayed such resolve was at the time of the Gulf War.

In the last months of 1990, as the U.S. was preparing for action, reporters from around the world interviewed those on "the Arab Street" who raged furiously at America and vowed perpetual allegiance to Saddam Hussein. Once Desert Storm had been launched, however, those same reporters and interviewees expressed thanks and support for the U.S. and confidence in its resolve and ultimate success. The world's people will make their obeisance to the strongman so long as, but only so long as, the U.S. shows a lack of resolve and staying power. Our actions must belie the impression gained in the Arab world and elsewhere in recent years that America "is short of breath."

An immense opportunity now exists to shape the war on terrorism to positive ends in view of the nature and extent of the terrorist threat to virtually every state in the world.

State is the key term and fundamental entity of international relations. The past decade has been marked by a widening belief that the sovereign state is on the way out; that the information revolution, international "civil society," globalization, and other inexorable forces of change are rendering the state obsolete.

Sovereignty, the state, international law, diplomacy, treaties, protocols, and conventions are all mechanisms bequeathed to us by the previous three or four centuries. They have been subjected to enormous stresses and strains in the past three or four decades. But just as a hard disk drive is an electromechanical device in the electronic age of the computer it makes effective, so the state remains the indispensable core entity of international life. Despite all the fond hopes and brainy theories of recent years, no replacement for the state is in sight. Not one of the array of problems of the new transborder agenda—climate change, AIDS, crime, pollution, human rights, the global economy, etc.—can be solved unless stable and responsible states agree to combine their efforts to address such problems.

The U.S. must help Arab regimes recognize that their commitment to their faith and to their people can best be strengthened through a commitment to the institution of the state. A more ideal form of government may be imaginable, but none is realizable in this era of the world's history.

Terrorism is the ultimate assault weapon against the state. So the new war on terrorism provides a natural bonding agent for today's states and the international states system that we trace back to the seventeenth century. This system remains the foundation-stone for all we do in the global arena. Nongovernmental organizations or other would-be rivals of the state cannot solve the world's problems.

A revitalized, state-centered, and clearly antiterrorist approach could advance the resolution of some of the world's intractable conflicts, almost all of which involve two communities unwilling to be part of one state. If terrorism can truly be suppressed, the fear that stands in the way of accommodation will be vastly diminished. It is the Irish Republican Army's terrorist arms that stand in the way of Ulster's incorporation into the state of Ireland. The new U.S. relationships with both India and Pakistan, compelled by a commitment to end terrorism, offer hope for progress on the problem of Kashmir. These and other conflicts cannot be closed out quickly or easily, but victory in the war on terrorism could transform the international scene in the cause of peace and stability.

8.

It will help in dispelling modern and insidious myths about terrorism and the Middle East if we were to revive an ancient and instructive one: defeating terrorism is like the twelve labors of Hercules—it requires patience, fortitude and the willingness and ability to undertake diverse and difficult tasks.

1. The first labor imposed on Hercules was to kill the Nemean Lion, a huge beast with skin impervious to weapons of stone, bronze, or iron. Finding that the high-technology weapons of his time were of no avail, Hercules had no choice but to wrestle the animal down. Our technological superiority is an invaluable advantage, but ultimately, in both intelligence and combat, there is no replacement for the human mind.

2. Each time Hercules struck off one of the many heads of the Hydra, replacement heads sprouted up, spewing venom in the air. Only by holding his breath while cauterizing the stumps of the heads could Hercules destroy the monster. We must simultaneously defend ourselves from biological and chemical attack, even as we dig out the roots of terror.

3. Next, Hercules needed to capture the Ceryneian Hind, without using the least force, and carry her on a long journey. The little deer was sacred to the goddess Artemis, who had to be convinced that the task was necessary. Careful and contin-

ual diplomatic work will be required to gain and keep support for the American effort over the long course of this war.

4. The vicious Erymanthian Boar was ravaging the countryside. To take it, Hercules needed to neutralize its enormous strength. This he did by maneuvering it into a deep snowdrift, where its power proved useless. Methods other than direct, main force will at times be necessary and may be most effective.

5. The filth in the Augean Stables was the accumulation of many years and spread a pestilence across the land. It was thought that Hercules would have to load the dung in baskets and carry it away one load at a time. Instead, he diverted mighty rivers to wash out the muck. The lesson for us is that for some tasks, the combined pressures of many nations will be needed to do the job right.

6. A miasmic swamp was the impenetrable refuge in which the murderous Stymphalian Birds bred. Occasionally they would take to the air in countless numbers to kill people with their knifelike talons, at the same time blighting the crops with poisonous excrement. Like Hercules, we will have to drain the swamp where the terrorists live and frighten them into the open, where they can be killed or captured.

7. Ordered to capture the Cretan Bull, Hercules subdued it after a long struggle, only to have the goddess Hera set it free. The properly constituted laws and procedures of justice must be respected.

8. King Diomedes kept four savage mares and fed them on the flesh of unsuspecting passersby. Hercules contrived to

turn them on the king himself and mastered them when they were thus distracted. Those who harbor terrorists must know that they too will be victims of terror.

9. The Amazon Queen Hippolyte chose to wear the belt of Mars. When she refused to give up the belt to Hercules, a pitched battle ensued. When Hippolyte was thrown from her horse, Hercules stood over her, club in hand, offering quarter, but the Amazon chose to die rather than yield. Those who commit acts of war will be warred upon until they surrender or die.

10. Forbidden to pay bribes or use threats, Hercules nonetheless rounded up the cattle of Geryon and herded them home. The aims of war can be achieved justly without violating fundamental principles.

11. After Hercules had performed these ten labors, taking several years to do so, he was given two more tasks. The eleventh was to gather fruit from the golden apple trees of Hesperides. Hercules turned to Atlas for assistance, offering to shoulder Atlas's global burden for him at this time. We cannot fight the war on terrorism alone. We will need the help of others and will have to help those who help us.

12. Hercules' last and most difficult labor was to confront Cerberus, the Hound of Hell. When Hercules gripped the dog by the throat, three heads rose up, each with a tangled mane of vipers, and the dog's barbed tail snapped to strike. Hercules survived, protected by the unique lion's pelt that he wore. If terrorists can turn airplanes into giant cruise missiles, what would happen if they had control over the nuclear

weapons and missiles of Pakistan? A missile defense system is indispensable not only for national defense, but also to enable the U.S. to take offensive action.

As everyone, starting with the president, has said, the new war on terrorism will take years to win. But the enemy has its own vulnerabilities, and many of our strengths are intact. The challenge is to apply them in a way that is not just heroic but that is strategic as well.

CHAPTER 5

CLASHING CIVILIZATIONS OR MAD MULLAHS: THE UNITED STATES BETWEEN INFORMAL AND FORMAL EMPIRE

Niall Ferguson

I.

On July 30, 1914, slowly realizing that Britain intended to declare war on Germany, the Emperor Wilhelm II seized on an idea with which he is seldom associated—jihad:

> ...Our consuls in Turkey, in India, agents etc., must fire the whole Mohammedan world to fierce rebellion against this hated, lying, conscienceless nation of shop-keepers; for if we are to be bled to death, England shall at least lose India.

The idea of the First World War as a holy war against the British Empire seems to us absurd. Indeed, it inspired one of the most far-fetched of wartime novels, John Buchan's *Greenmantle* (1916). Yet recent research has revealed that the

Germans did indeed seek to "fire the whole Mohammedan world" during the First World War. Three and a half months later, in the presence of Germany's new ally, the Ottoman sultan, the Sheikh-ul-Islam issued a fatwa that declared an Islamic holy war against Britain and her allies. Swiftly translated into Arabic, Persian, Urdu and Tatar, it was addressed to both Shiite and Sunni Muslims. Given that roughly 120 million of the world's 270 Muslims lived under British, French or Russian rule, this was indeed a potentially revolutionary call to arms.

Talk of "World War III" in the immediate aftermath of September 11, brought all this to mind. So too did the widespread praise of Samuel Huntington for his prescience in predicting a new "clash of civilizations" back in 1993.

In times of crisis, historians are expected to find illuminating parallels with past crises. In the aftermath of September 11 not all have been able to oblige. The distinguished British military historian John Keegan all but admitted defeat in the London *Spectator*:

> During the Falklands and Gulf wars I could help. History supplied all sorts of clues as to what was happening and what the outcome would be. The nasties made familiar mistakes. One could state with confidence how they would go wrong and why our side would win. This time, stop me. Not even the Mongols—about the nastiest enemies civilization has ever had to face—took war to the extreme of killing themselves so as to kill others.

Yet this seems too hasty an abdication. For the German holy war is only one of many intriguing past episodes that help shed light on the present. Even less well-known, but equally relevant as I write, is the fact that the Germans sought to use anthrax in the First World War, sending agents abroad to infect cattle and horses intended for import to Britain. As for Keegan's baffling enemy who "kill themselves so as to kill others," that seems a fair description of the five thousand Japanese pilots who killed themselves flying kamikaze ("divine wind") missions in 1944 and 1945.

On reflection, there are precedents for nearly all the elements of the attacks of September 11; the only real novelty was their *combination*. Consider simply the mechanics of the operation. Apart from its kamikaze character, it was essentially a multiple hijacking. This form of air piracy is certainly not new: since the late 1960s, when the tactic first began to be used systematically by the Palestine Liberation Organization and its sympathizers, there have been more than five hundred hijackings. Similarly, the effect of crashing two aircraft into the World Trade Center bears close comparison with the effect of any successful bombing of a major conurbation. Since their devastating use by both sides in the Second World War, such aerial attacks on cities have in fact been a central component of warfare and were quickly resorted to by NATO itself during the 1999 war against the rump Yugoslavia.

Even the way the attacks on New York and Washington were relayed by the modern media to the rest of the world has parallels in the past. During the Luftwaffe's Blitz against London in 1940–41 Ed Murrow, CBS's bureau chief in London, was able to relay his impressions to tens of thousands of American listeners. "You burnt the city of London in our homes," wrote the poet Archibald MacLeish of Murrow's radio broadcasts, "and we felt the flames."

It is, of course, tempting to say that on September 11, Americans themselves "felt the flames" for the first time. The U.S. had scarcely any experience of being the direct target of international terrorism until that day. Between 1995 and 2000, according to State Department figures, there were around 2,129 international terrorist attacks; just 15 of them occurred in North America, causing just seven casualties. On the other hand, U.S. citizens abroad have been terrorist targets for years: a further 70 Americans were killed and 651 wounded by terrorist attacks outside the U.S. in the course of the past five years. And of course, a domestic act of terrorism—the Oklahoma bombing—starkly revealed to Americans the devastating possibilities of urban terrorism six years ago.

But what of the motive? Was it not strange that those responsible for the attack made no specific demands in its aftermath? Hardly. Readers of Conrad's *Secret Agent* may recall the words of the sinister Slav diplomat Mr. Vladimir, the subversive mastermind who plots to bomb the Greenwich Observatory as one of a "series of outrages" to be "executed here in this country." "These outrages," Vladimir explains to his intended bomber, the hapless Verloc, "must be sufficiently startling—effective. Let them be directed against buildings, for instance.... The attack must have all the shocking senselessness of gratuitous blasphemy...[it must be] the most alarming display of ferocious imbecility." It must, in short, be a symbolic act: one that speaks for itself. "What is the fetish of the hour that all the bourgeoisie recognize—eh, Mr Verloc?" Vladimir asks. A hundred years ago the "fetish of the hour" was science—hence Vladimir's decision to attack the observatory. Today, of course, the fetish is economic globalization—hence the targeting of the World Trade Center.

Nor was Conrad merely letting his imagination run riot. The anarchist terrorism that inspired him was a reality. Since the 1860s, men like the Russian anarchist Sergei Nechaev had been preaching a doctrine of terrorism in which violence—notionally to further "the revolution"—came close to becoming an end in itself. It was Nechaev who wrote *Principles of Revolution*, which grimly declared, "We recognize no other activity but the work of extermination." As far as his tactics are concerned, Osama bin Laden owes a bigger debt to the nineteenth-century Russian nihilists and *narodniki* than he does to the CIA.

The obvious objection is that there is a profound difference between pre-1900 nihilism and the Islamic fundamentalism espoused by bin Laden and his al Qaeda organization. Yet it would be a grave mistake to overstate that difference. One of the dangers of Huntington's "clash of civilizations" thesis is that it exaggerates the homogeneity of Islam as a world religion. It might be more illuminating to regard al

Qaeda as the extremist wing of a *political religion*, a term recently and illuminatingly used by the historian Michael Burleigh to capture the nature of Nazism. The defining characteristics of a political religion are the pursuit of worldly goals—for example, the ejection of the United States from Saudi Arabia, or the destruction of the state of Israel— through messianic leadership and mass indoctrination. On that basis, al Qaeda has more in common with other extreme organizations, including those from quite different cultural milieus, than with the "mainstream" Islam of relatively secularized countries like Turkey or Morocco, to say nothing of the immigrant Muslim communities of the West.

That is not to imply, as some writers on the left have hastened to claim, that al Qaeda, or indeed the Taliban regime, represents some kind of "Islamo-fascism" (a term first used by Christopher Hitchens in *The Nation*). The fascist movements of the 1920s and 30s were never especially adept at terrorism, preferring to seize control of existing nation-states and to make war using conventional military forces. "Islamo-nihilism" would be nearer the mark, or perhaps "Islamo-bolshevism"—for we should not forget that in their early years Lenin and Stalin were also terrorists in the Nechaevian tradition. Indeed, there is more than a passing resemblance between "Hereditary Nobleman Ulyanov," as the young Lenin liked to style himself, hatching his plans for the overthrow of tsarism from dingy Swiss hotels, and the renegade Saudi millionaire orchestrating mayhem from an Afghan cave.

Nor should we forget that "Western civilization"—by which Huntington presumably means the distinctive Protestant-Deist-Catholic-Jewish mix that underpins today's American public life—has itself been capable of producing political religions just as intolerant and bloodthirsty as today's Islamo-bolshevism. It may not be very tactful to point it out at this juncture, but the Pilgrim Fathers themselves were the products of a militant Puritanism that went on to wage a violent revolutionary war in Britain in the 1640s. Before September 11, critics of the Taliban regime habitually lamented its misogyny, iconoclasm and bloody penal code. Yet Western Europe in the seventeenth century—the very cradle of Huntington's beloved Western civilization—was a hotbed of witch-burning, altar smashing and public disemboweling. Presumably, too, the American Revolution was as much a product of Western civilization as its French counterpart, an event that gave the word terror its modern political meaning.

2.

What, then, of the target of the present war? Does history offer any parallels for the situation the United States currently finds itself in? The answer is that it offers several—provided we recognize that the United States is a mature, and in some respects decadent, empire.

In his *Decline and Fall of the Roman Empire*, Edward Gibbon described a confrontation between just such an empire and a new political religion not once but twice. In his famous (once notorious) fifteenth chapter, the greatest of all historians portrayed early Christianity itself as the radical sect that began to undermine the might of an already corrupt Rome. He painted a very similar picture of the role played by early Islam in overthrowing Byzantium in his less well-known fiftieth chapter. Another, more recent parallel that suggests itself is with the Habsburg Empire at the time of Charles V and his successors, who had to contend with the new fundamentalism of the Reformation from the moment in 1517 when Luther nailed up his ninety-five theses in Wittenberg.

Those comparisons, however, may exaggerate the potential threat posed by today's Islamo-bolshevism and understate the power of the United States to defend itself. Perhaps a more illuminating comparison is with another empire that was at, or had perhaps just passed, its zenith just a hundred years ago: that of Great Britain. The parallel is not exact, of course, but it offers at least some insight into where we may be heading.

True, no one today would be so crass as to call occupying and governing Afghanistan "the White Man's burden." Even the British Prime Minister Tony Blair's messianic speech at the Labour Party conference on October 3 talked innocuously about "partnership," "the politics of globalization" and "reordering the world." Yet the content of that speech was pure Kipling—albeit translated into politically correct language for the benefit of his congenitally anti-imperialist audience.

The new imperialism in fact predates the war in Afghanistan by some years. A precedent was set in the

Balkans, largely forgotten in all the excitement of this new conflict. Only six years ago, in 1995, the West intervened to bring a stop to the war in Bosnia. Two years ago we intervened again to halt the "ethnic cleansing" of Kosovo. Today, in the aftermath of our military action, Bosnia and Kosovo are being administered as colonies in all but name by international organizations backed by American and European soldiers—some 50,000 NATO troops in the case of Kosovo. Nor are these the only "neo-colonies." There is also what amounts to a UN protectorate in East Timor, while the stability of Sierra Leone continues to depend on the presence of the small but highly effective British military force deployed in May last year. Indeed, one of the most surreal sights of the new millennium was that of a crowd in Freetown cheering the (re)imposition of British rule.

According to Mr. Blair, none of this counts as imperialism because we have gone into these places not to exploit them economically (as in the bad old days) but to prevent them either from harboring terrorism or from menacing their neighbors. We are, he argues, "bringing" such countries democracy and freedom. But that is not all. We give them aid, write off their debts, "help with good governance and infrastructure," train their soldiers in "conflict resolution" and encourage investment and access to our markets. In return, all they have to do is give up "bad governance" and "abuses of human rights." What could be more reasonable—indeed, altruistic?

Two things about this are noteworthy. The first is that

there is obviously something deeply paradoxical about *imposing* democracy and freedom on a country. The second is that the "deal" Mr. Blair describes is not a new kind of colonialism at all. It is almost exactly what the late-Victorian generation of British imperialists said they were doing. Indeed, that is the whole point of Kipling's poem "The White Man's Burden."

Although there is no question that the British Empire had its origins in the more or less unqualified pursuit of profit, by the nineteenth century it had evolved a rhetoric of high-mindedness that, quite unconsciously, Mr. Blair and the other neo-imperialists are echoing. Thus, when the British went to war against the Sudan in the 1880s and 90s, they had no doubt that they were imposing the values of civilization on what we would now call a "rogue state." The Mahdi was in many ways a Victorian Osama bin Laden, a renegade Islamic fundamentalist whose murder of General Gordon in January 1885 was the "September 11" of the era. In the same way, the Battle of Omdurman in 1898—when Kitchener's Maxim guns mowed down 10,000 of the Mahdi's followers—was the prototype for the kinds of war the U.S. has been fighting since 1990, beginning in Kuwait and now under way in Afghanistan.

Nor do the parallels end there. Just as the U.S. Air Force bombed Serbia in 1999 in the name of "human rights," so the Royal Navy conducted raids on the West African coast in the 1840s and even threatened Brazil as part of a highly moralistic campaign to end the slave trade. And just as Mr.

Blair justifies his "ethical imperialism" by promising its beneficiaries aid, good governance and infrastructure—not to
mention military training—so his liberal predecessor
William Gladstone justified the military occupation of
Egypt in 1881. Even our modern disdain for the Taliban
regime's treatment of women recalls the way British admin-
istrators in India strove to stamp out the customs of suttee
(the burning of widows on their husbands' funeral pyres)
and female infanticide.

What lessons can the United States today learn from the
British experience of empire? The obvious one is that the
most successful economy in the world—as Britain was for
much of the eighteenth and nineteenth centuries—can do a
very great deal to impose its preferred values on less technologically advanced societies. It is nothing short of astonishing
that Great Britain was able to govern around a quarter of the
world's population and land surface—and nearly all of its
oceans—without running up an especially large defense bill.
(To be precise, Britain's defense expenditure averaged just 3.1
percent of net national product between 1870 and 1913, and
it was lower for the rest of the nineteenth century.) This was
despite the fact that Britain fought 72 separate military cam-
paigns in the course of Queen Victoria's reign—more than
one for every year of the so-called *pax britannica*.

This was money well spent. No doubt it is true that, in
theory, open international commerce would have been
preferable to imperialism; but in practice global free trade
has not been naturally occurring. It has been claimed by

the British economic historian Patrick O'Brien that, after around 1846, Britain could have withdrawn from empire with impunity and reaped a "decolonization dividend" in the form of a 25 percent tax cut. Yet the challenges to British hegemony from protectionist rivals were in many ways greater in the late 19th and early 20th centuries than in any previous period. Abandoning formal control over Britain's colonies would almost certainly have led to higher tariffs being erected against British exports in their markets, and perhaps other forms of trade discrimination. The evidence for this need not be purely hypothetical: it is manifest in the highly protectionist policies adopted by the United States and India after they secured independence, as well as in the tariffs erected by Britain's imperial rivals—France, Germany and Russia—between 1878 and 1914. Britain's military budget before the First World War can therefore be seen as a remarkably low economical insurance premium against international protectionism. And the economic benefit of enforcing free trade could have been as high as 6.5 percent of GNP. In short, empire paid a real dividend.

By comparison, the United States today is vastly wealthier than the rest of the world than Britain ever was. In 1913 Britain's share of total world output was 8.3 percent; the equivalent figure for the U.S. in 1998 was 21.9 percent. Nor should anybody pretend that, at least in fiscal terms, the cost of expanding the American empire—even if it were to mean a great many little wars like the one currently underway—

would be prohibitive. Last year American defense spending stood at just 2.9 percent of GNP, compared with an average for the years 1948–1998 of 6.8 percent.

The hypothesis, in other words, is a step in the direction of *political* globalization, with the United States shouldering "the White Man's burden" as late-Victorian Britain once did. That is certainly what we should expect if history repeats itself. Like the United States today, Britain did not set out to rule 25 percent of the world's land surface. Its empire began as a network of coastal bases and economic spheres of influence, much like the post-1945 American "empire." But real and perceived threats to British commercial interests constantly tempted the British to progress from informal to formal imperialism. That was how so much of the atlas of 1901 came to be colored imperial pink.

Yet there are good reasons to doubt that a similar transition is now under way in the American case. On close inspection, America's strengths may not be the strengths of a natural imperial hegemon. For one thing, British imperial power relied on the massive export of capital and people. But since 1972 the American economy has been a net *im*porter of capital (to the tune of 17 percent of gross national product last year), and it remains the favored destination of immigrants from around the world, not a producer of would-be colonial emigrants. Moreover, Britain in its heyday was able to draw on a culture of unabashed imperialism that dated back to the Elizabethan period; whereas the U.S.—born not in a war against slavery (as Mr. Blair claimed in his conference speech) but in a war against the British Empire—will always be a reluctant ruler of other peoples.

In 1913 there was a revealing conversation on this subject between the British Foreign Secretary, Sir Edward Grey, and the American ambassador to London, Walter Page, following a coup in Mexico.

"Suppose you have to intervene, what then?" asked Grey.

"Make 'em vote and live by their decisions," replied the American.

"But suppose they will not so live?"

"We'll go in and make 'em vote again."

"And keep this up for 200 years?" asked Grey.

"Yes," replied the ambassador. "The United States... can continue to shoot men for that little space till they learn to vote and to rule themselves."

That, it might be said, has been the recurrent theme of American foreign policy for too long: drop some bombs, march in, then hold elections and get the hell out—until the next crisis. Haiti is the classic example. The obvious danger is that something similar may happen in the wake of this latest war. Because the United States is so reluctant to rule any foreign territory directly, there will be a rush to install a supposedly democratic regime followed by another, less dignified rush for the exits. The same thing would already have happened in Kosovo by now if it were not so obvious that the Albanians would slaughter the Serbs the moment we left.

It is easily forgotten, but only a few months ago many American security experts were urging the United States not to increase but to reduce her overseas commitments. Indeed, the strong implication of early statements by President Bush's national security adviser Condoleezza Rice and Secretary of State Colin Powell was that the new administration intended to scale down the deployment of U.S. forces overseas. As Powell put it, "Our armed forces are stretched rather thin, and there is a limit to how many of these deployments we can sustain." This is hardly the language of neo-colonialism.

3.

If the hypothesis is political globalization, then the antithesis is fragmentation—*de*globalization, if you like.

There is certainly a risk of a political backlash against globalization. Harold James has recently argued that what happened in the 1930s—when the free movements of capital, goods and labor all but ceased—could conceivably repeat itself. As James shows, the Great Depression can be understood as a kind of reaction against the pre-1914 era of globalization. Even before the First World War, some governments were raising tariffs and restricting immigration. Then, in the 1920s, the system of free trade and international monetary integration (the gold standard) fell into disrepute, and along with it all the fledgling institutions of political "internationalism" that had sprung up after the war. No one made more political capital out of the failure of globalization than Hitler. During his barnstorming election campaign of July 1932 he asked German voters a telling question:

> There's so much internationalism, so much world con-
> science, so many international contracts; there's the League
> of Nations, the Disarmament Conference, Moscow, the
> Second International, the Third International—and what
> did all that produce for Germany?

What they all produced in the end was, of course, Hitler himself.

Yet the risk of a complete unraveling of economic global-ization seems lower today than it was on the eve of the Great Depression. Admittedly, the world economy was already slowing down even before September 11 as the long boom of the Clinton years petered out. The "new economic para-digm" was dead, the productivity miracle buried with it and the trade cycle dancing on their grave. In the immediate aftermath of the attacks, investors had to grit their teeth as stocks threatened to go into free fall—at one point the Dow Jones Industrial index was more than 40 percent off its January 2001 peak. Yet so far the deflation of the late 1990s asset price bubble has been a gentle affair compared to the cataclysm that followed the bubble of the 1920s. (To give some orders of magnitude, a crash on the 1929–32 scale would take the Dow down from over 11,723—where it stood at its peak in January last year—to around 1,266 by

November next year. At the time of writing [October 2001], it stands at 9,163. When Alan Greenspan coined the phrase "irrational exuberance," the index was a mere 6,473.)

There are three reasons to remain hopeful that a second Great Depression can be avoided. First, the structure of American and European banking is a great deal healthier than was the case seventy years ago. Second, the international monetary system is more flexible, thanks to the combination of floating exchange rates and huge foreign exchange markets, which enable companies to hedge against currency movements. Finally, we must recognize how much harder it is to disrupt the globalization of communications, which was such an integral part of the 1990s boom. In the 1930s it was still possible for authoritarian governments more or less to cut off their citizens from uncensored media or foreign contacts. Newspapers, radio, and cinema could effectively be monopolized and manipulated; letters to and from abroad could simply be opened; international travel was the preserve of a minority. Apart from the fact that it was possible (though illegal) to pick up the BBC on certain kinds of radio receivers, Germans in the Third Reich had only the haziest notion of what was going on in the world outside.

Today, by contrast, only a few governments in very backward countries can exert this kind of control over communications. Satellites and the Internet really have created a new world of borderless information flows. And even if it were possible to terrorize Americans away from flying, opening their mail and even using the Internet (imagine a devastating computer virus), other channels of global communication would still remain open.

4.

The real question is not so much of economic deglobalization as of continued political fragmentation. For one of the great ironies of our time is that the economic integration of the world has coincided with its political disintegration.

Excluding sub-Saharan Africa, there were 64 independent countries in the world in 1871. Forty-three years later, on the eve of the First World War, imperialism had reduced the number to 59. But since the Second World War there have been sustained increases. In 1946 there were 74 independent countries; in 1950, 89. By 1995 the number was 192, with the two biggest increases coming in the 1960s (mainly Africa, where 25 new states were formed between 1960 and 1964) and the 1990s (mainly Eastern Europe). Moreover, many of the new states are tiny. At least 87 of today's states have fewer than 5 million inhabitants, 58 have fewer than 2.5 million and 35 have fewer than 500,000. More than half of the world's countries have fewer inhabitants than the state of Massachusetts.

It could perhaps be suggested that this appearance of political fragmentation conceals contrary growth in the power of supranational institutions: that is indeed a common complaint of those antiglobalization protesters whose noisy demonstrations have suddenly come to seem so trivial. The more utopian internationalists—and the more paranoid of conspiracy theorists—look forward, with eagerness and dread respectively, to an era of world government under the auspices of the United Nations, which will extend its original mandate to include the defense of human rights, regardless of national sovereignty.

There is, however, a difficulty with this scenario, and that is the fundamental financial weakness of most supranational organizations. In financial terms, these behemoths—including the biggest of all, the United Nations—are midgets. The total operating expenses of the UN, the World Bank, the IMF and all UN programs and agencies amounted to $18.2 billion a year in 1999. The U.S. federal budget was approximately a hundred times larger. The same kind of calculation should be borne in mind when the idea is floated that the European Union could become a federal "super-state." The European Union's total expenditure in 1999 was little more than 1 percent of total European GDP; expenditure by national governments accounted for around 48 percent. Global purchasing power remains concentrated in the hands of the nation-states.

In this context, the main significance of movements like Islamic fundamentalism may lie in their centrifugal rather than centripetal effects. Rather than anticipating a clash between monolithic civilizations, we should expect a continued process of disintegration as religious and ethnic conflicts challenge the integrity of existing multicultural nation-states. Civil war has, after all, been the most frequent kind of war since 1945: something like two-thirds of all postwar conflicts have been within, rather than between, states. From Yugoslavia to Iraq to Afghanistan, what the United States keeps having to confront these days is not a united Islam but a succession of fractured polities, racked by internecine war. The same could be said about Somalia, Sierra Leone and Rwanda.

Why has economic globalization coincided with political fragmentation in this contradictory fashion? One possible answer is that global market forces increase regional inequalities inside traditional nation states. Another is that the superficial homogenization of popular culture—through Hollywood, the pop music industry, and the Anglicization of technical communication—promotes an accentuation of local identities as a kind of a bloody-minded reaction. But the best answer may be that as more and more states adopt (with American encouragement) a combination of economic openness and political democracy, the rationale of many multiethnic states falls away. Central government loses its legitimacy as the planner of the economy, and ethnic groups vote for separatist parties. This process of political fission has not yet run its historic course.

5.

What we are witnessing, then, is not a clash of civilizations but a collision between a mature empire and a dynamic and dangerous political religion, in a world that is as politically fissiparous as it is economically integrated. That is why talk of World War III is so misleading. The Second World War *was* a clash of civilizations: the Anglophone democracies, the ultra-nationalist Axis powers and the communist Soviet Union. What made the clash so spectacular was that the civilizations in question proved so evenly matched in terms of their capacity to mete out destruction.

What lies ahead for the United States is something quite different. Like the British Empire a century ago, America has unrivalled economic and military resources. Indeed, her position is in some ways better, as no rival great power poses as imminent a threat as Germany did to Britain after 1900. But she feels herself to be—in Matthew Arnold's words—a "weary Titan, struggling under the too vast orb of its fate." Her impulse is to cling to "splendid isolation" (another late-Victorian phrase) and to spend her resources not on stealth bombers but on SUVs. Yet self-sufficiency is not an option, for there are mad mullahs today with vastly more firepower than the original "Mad Mullah"—Mohammed bin Abdullah Hassan, against whom the British had to fight a prolonged desert war in Somaliland between 1901 and 1919. In effect, it might be said, the Mad Mullah has joined forces with Conrad's Mr. Vladimir.

In my book *The Cash Nexus*, I made the argument that the United States not only could afford to play a more assertive global role; it could not afford *not* to. In this context it might be worth reiterating several important components of the argument.

1. *The U.S. ceased to be invulnerable long before September 11.*
Writing back in late 2000, I thought it highly unlikely that
any state would contemplate a direct attack on the U.S. in
the foreseeable future, but I did warn that "a terrorist campaign against American cities is quite easy to imagine." Now
imagination is not necessary.

2. *The means of destruction have never been cheaper.* In particular, the Soviet practice of systematically underpricing defense
goods has left an enduring legacy of cheap weaponry, the
main beneficiaries of which have been and remain the guerrilla armies of the Middle East and sub-Saharan Africa, the
terrorist groups of Western Europe and the drug gangs of the
Americas. At the time I wrote the book, a used AK-47 assault
rifle could be purchased in the United States for $700, a new
one for $1,395—almost exactly as much as the cost of the
portable computer on which this chapter was written. In the
same way, the real cost of a nuclear warhead—and certainly
the real cost of a kiloton of nuclear yield—is lower today than
at any time since the Manhattan Project achieved its goal at a
cost of $2 billion in 1945 dollars. Converted into prices of
1993, that figure rises tenfold: enough to buy four hundred
Trident II missiles. It seems reasonable to assume that the
same process has reduced the cost of weapons of biological
warfare such as refined anthrax. This kind of immensely
destructive weaponry is getting more affordable—not just for
legitimate states but also for insurgents who wish to intensify
civil wars and for terrorists who wish to strike at the United
States or its allies. The implication is clear: what happened on

September 11 may prove to have been just a foretaste of far worse death and destruction still to come.

3. *Global inequality has risen significantly, and with it dissatisfaction among the losers.* There can be little doubt that the lopsided nature of economic globalization—the fact that capital flows mainly within the developed world, that trade and migration are still restricted in many ways—is leading to unprecedented levels of inequality around the world. In the 1960s the richest fifth of the world's population had a total income thirty times greater than the poorest fifth's; in 1998 the ratio was 74:1. In 1965 real GDP per capita in Chad was one-*fifteenth* of the U.S. figure; in 1990 it was one-*fiftieth*. If the first age of globalization saw a substantial measure of convergence of incomes, this age is seeing a pronounced divergence. This kind of inequality is likely to increase the resentment felt in poorer countries toward the U.S.

4. *The United Nations is incapable of coping with the challenge of global disorder without strong U.S. leadership.* Besides terrorism, the most common international problem in the foreseeable future is likely to be civil war, for reasons already discussed. But the United Nations is not an institution capable of effective peacemaking in civil wars. Between 1992 and 1999, the Security Council authorized a series of humanitarian interventions in Somalia, Bosnia, Rwanda, Haiti, Cambodia, Albania and East Timor. The last of these operations was successful; but the rest were at best ineffective, and at worst disastrous. The fiasco of the U.S. Rangers mission to Mogadishu in 1993, the abject failure of the Security

Council to reinforce the French contingent in Rwanda in 1994 and the Dutch impotence and possible complicity in the massacre at Srebrenica in 1995—these episodes have cast grave doubt on the ability of the UN to react rapidly and effectively enough to crises. Nothing illustrates more clearly the limits of the power of supranational institutions than the events of 1999. Because Kosovo was (and remains) an integral province of Serbia, the Yugoslav government was legally protected from external intervention by Article 2(4) of the UN Charter, which states that "all Members shall refrain… from the threat or use of force against the territorial integrity or political independence of any State;" and by Article 2(7), which prohibits intervention "in matters which are essentially within the domestic jurisdiction of any state." It was also covered by the General Assembly's 1970 Declaration on Principles of International Law, which denies members "the right to intervene, directly or indirectly, for any reason whatever, in the internal external affairs of any other state." Under the UN Charter, force may be used only in self-defense or with the explicit authorization of the Security Council in response to an act of aggression (Article 51 and Chapter III). No such authorization could be obtained in 1999 because of Russian opposition on the Security Council. True, it has been a different story since September 11. But, in practice the most the UN has been able to do has been to get its Afghan mission out of the way of U.S. air strikes, step up its relief efforts on the Afghan border and make nice-sounding plans for a post-Taliban democratic regime.

5. *Even after big defense cuts, the United States is still the world's only superpower*, with an unrivalled financial and military-technological capability. Its defense budget is fourteen times that of China and twenty-two times that of Russia. A further question, however, is whether or not any state is capable of attacking one of America's *allies*, or indeed of using violence anywhere in the world where American interests are at stake. In this context, it is significant that while the United States, Europe and the countries of the former Soviet Union have been disarming since the mid-1980s, other parts of the world have been rearming. According to the Stockholm International Peace Research Institute, arms exports to Northeast Asia and the Middle East have risen significantly since 1994. Some Asian powers now possess a nuclear capability (China, India and Pakistan), while Iraq continues to resist international efforts to curb its chemical and biological weapons program. The Pentagon estimates that at least twenty countries possess either short- or medium-range ballistic missiles.

6. *The U.S. needs to do more to impose order on rogue states.* The idea of invading a country, deposing its dictators and imposing the rule of law at gunpoint is usually dismissed as incompatible with American values. A common argument is that the U.S. could never engage in the kind of overt imperial rule practiced by Britain in the nineteenth century. Yet it is often forgotten that this was precisely what was done in Germany and in Japan at the end of the Second World War, and with great and lasting success. Charles Maier has argued

persuasively that American policy after 1945 *was* a form of imperialism, not different in essence from the European imperialisms of the nineteenth century, based on domestic political consensus, mastery of new communications technology and the export of a particular political economic model (corporatism based on raising productivity). In a similar vein, Robert Gilpin has maintained that Western economies only flourished after 1945 because they were underwritten by American military power. The trouble is that this kind of informal American imperialism has been in decline in recent years. Consider the fact that the U.S. currently spends just 0.1 percent of GDP on overseas development aid, or the fact that the Bush administration's top defense priority before September 11 was to develop a National Missile Defense system, a project that would appear to contravene the 1972 Anti-Ballistic Missiles Treaty. These are the symptoms of a deep-rooted insularity which is the very reverse of what the world needs from its wealthiest power.

7. *America can afford formal empire.* Far from retreating like some giant snail behind an electronic shell, the U.S. should be devoting a larger percentage of its vast resources to making the world safe for capitalism and democracy. Contrary to the naïve triumphalism of the "end of history," neither of these is naturally occurring; both require strong institutional foundations of law and order. The proper role of an imperial America is to establish these institutions where they are lacking, if necessary—as in Germany and Japan in 1945—by military force. There is no economic argument against such a

policy, since it would not be prohibitively costly. Imposing democracy on all the world's "rogue states" would not push the U.S. defense budget much above 5 percent of GDP. There is also an economic argument for doing so, as establishing the rule of law in such countries would pay a long-run dividend as their trade revived and expanded.

I concluded *The Cash Nexus* with a sentence I would now like to rephrase. Then, writing in the dying days of the Clinton administration, I wrote:

> The reasons this [i.e. a more "imperial" American foreign policy towards rogue states] will not happen are threefold: an ideological embarrassment about being seen to wield imperial power; an exaggerated notion of what Russia and China would do in response; and a pusillanimous fear of military casualties. Perhaps that is the greatest disappointment facing the world in the twenty-first century: that the leaders of the one state with the economic resources to make the world a better place lack the guts to do it.

I think that should now be a blunt question: "Do the leaders of the one state with the economic resources to make the world a better place have the guts to do it?"

We shall soon see.

CHAPTER 6

PRESERVING AMERICAN VALUES: THE CHALLENGE AT HOME AND ABROAD

Harold Hongju Koh

S EPTEMBER 11 SHOOK all of us to the core—no matter how close or how far we were from Ground Zero, no matter how many degrees of separation between us and the victims or bereaved. For individual citizens, everyday activities suddenly seemed dangerous as never before. For the nation as a whole, our sense of invulnerability was forever shattered, and our confidence about the future sharply shaken.

The terrorists attacked more than the symbols of U.S. economic and military strength—they struck at the very nature of our society and the qualities that have made us strong at home and influential abroad. They were trying to provoke us into a spasm of vengeance and intolerance comparable to their own. All the more reason, then, that even as we defend our security, we ensure the preservation of the universal values they sought to undermine—democracy, rule of law, human rights and an open society.

In the last half century, each of these has come to be recognized not simply as American or Western values, but as
universal ones, with internationally recognized meaning and
appeal. As the United Nations has acknowledged in a series
of resolutions, democracy means not just holding free and
fair elections, but governmental respect for such human
rights as the right to political participation and dissent; freedom of religion and belief; protection of minorities from
oppressive majority rule; and full respect for women's and
workers' rights in a civil society that includes independent
media and open, competitive economic structures. Rule of
law connotes governance not by the caprice of individuals,
but by legal norms shaped by constitutionalism, democrati-
cally elected political institutions, and an independent judici-
ary. International human rights embrace those universally
recognized inalienable rights to whose enjoyment all persons
are entitled solely by virtue of being born human. These were
universally accepted in the 1993 Vienna Human Rights
Declaration, and were articulated in the Universal Declaration
of Human Rights, and the International Covenants on Civil
and Political and Economic, Social and Cultural Rights. And
an open society means a pluralistic and liberal social order, in
which exercises of individual and group rights are broadly
tolerated. Taken together, these principles now form the basis
for an emerging global culture of democracy.

I.

The September 11 attacks have put at risk the positive aspect of globalization—a word and a concept that were controversial before September 11, and even more so since then. In recent years, we have endured a blizzard of words about the integrating effect of expanding and accelerating communication, finance, transportation, health and markets. Globalization has created new universal languages of cyberspace, law, trade, and money and has strikingly diminished the importance of borders. But of all the global trends, the most important has also been the most overlooked: the globalization of freedom and self-government—the expansion of democratic governance from some 22 countries half a century ago to about 120 today. At the beginning of the new millennium, an astonishing 63 percent of the people on the planet lived under some form of democratic rule.

But globalization has always had a negative aspect as well. The greater freedom that has come with the collapse of authoritarianism has also left criminals and terrorists at liberty to move around the world with greater ease and speed. On September 11, we saw these forces turn the very mobility and openness of our society against us. Our challenge has thus become how to use the constructive face of globalization to overcome its most destructive face.

Over the past thirty years, the U.S. has supported the spread of freedom and democracy on the theory that they help provide humane solutions to the problems of the modern world: international environmental degradation, the AIDS crisis, cross-border crime and drug smuggling, trafficking in persons, and gross and systematic human rights violations. September 11 has now riveted our attention as never before on the threat of transnational terrorism.

We cannot depict this struggle as a clash of civilizations or as a battle between the West and Islam. Rather, it is a battle between those who support the emerging global culture of democracy—the post-cold war version of the "Free World"—and those who support global terrorism, recently defined by the United Nations General Assembly as "criminal acts intended or calculated to provoke a state of terror in the general public, a group of persons or particular persons for political purposes... whatever the considerations of a political, philosophical, ideological, racial, ethnic, religious or other nature that may be invoked to justify them."

Plainly, this is not a fight we can win by ourselves. As with the strategy we used in World War II to save democracy from fascism, we need to mobilize the forces of democracy to build a durable coalition against terrorism that will hang together to achieve our long-term goals.

Maintaining that coalition will be hard work. As the U.S. demonstrated when evicting Saddam Hussein from Kuwait in the Gulf War and evicting Slobodan Milosevic from Kosovo, to sustain a coalition we must rally and lead our allies, not bully them. In the spirit of democracy, we must listen to our allies, not just make demands of them. We must avoid quid pro quo coalition-building in favor of deeper alliances. Each country should commit itself to battle global terrorism not simply because it might be the next victim, but because it has just as much stake as we do in the global system of free transport, communication, markets and open societies that the terrorists have put in jeopardy.

In designing our strategy, we must deploy the full range of our foreign policy tools. First and most obviously, deliberate and carefully targeted use of military force will be a critical and necessary element of the strategy. But Vietnam taught us that we cannot win an unconventional war with conventional methods or declare all-out war against a shadow aggressor without rules, concern for civilian casualties, or an exit strategy. Nor should the overused analogy to Pearl Harbor mislead us into thinking that the most appropriate response is massive military force. In designing our response, what is most massive may not be most effective.

What this means, second, is that the application of force and vigorous resort to diplomacy must go hand in glove: force must be backed by creative diplomacy and creative diplomacy must be backed by effective force. To build an effective coalition, we need energetic diplomacy to line up support not just from our traditional partners—NATO, the United Nations, the G-8, the Organization of American States—but also from the Islamic Conference, the Organization of African Unity, and the Association of Southeast Asian Nations. Third, we must use economic sanctions and enlist the aid of such private entities as corporations, banks, nongovernmental organizations, and the media to trace and freeze the financial assets that these terrorist networks and their state supporters use. Fourth, while this may not be solely a law enforcement problem, neither does calling it a "war" eliminate the need for aggressive counterintelligence and law enforcement techniques. Terrorist acts have been committed by international criminals who belong to an international criminal network that uses textbook criminal techniques. Time-tested methods of law enforcement remain the best tools to bring those criminals to justice.

Fifth, we need to work not just with democratic governments, but also with the forces of democratization within even the most despotic countries. Some have blithely spoken of "ending" states that support terrorism. But countries are not monoliths. In my time working on the promotion of human rights and democracy for the State Department, I learned that in every state—including Afghanistan and Iraq—there are forces of democratization and forces of terror. Just take a look at Serbia. Only a little over a year ago, Slobodan Milosevic reigned by terror; then, suddenly, he was toppled in a peaceful transition and replaced by the democratic government of President Kostunica.

If we are to have any chance of ending for all time the practice of states harboring terrorists, we need to promote democratic transitions in those countries by supporting the indigenous, law-abiding, civil society groups who would pursue a different path. In so doing, we need to use carrots and not just sticks. We need to offer foreign and development aid and to consider measures such as debt relief for the countries who need it most. We need to keep up our democracy-building and rule-of-law programs, not just in those Middle Eastern and Central Asian countries whose help we will need for this antiterrorism struggle, but also in other parts of the world (especially Africa) where democracy remains weak and peace remains fragile. In the months ahead, what we choose to do *with* these foreign countries will be far more important than what we choose to do *to* them.

Finally, we must recognize that the assault on globalization we saw on September 11 represents only the most violent and virulent strain of the antiglobalization sentiment seen in far more benign forms in Seattle, Genoa, Prague, and elsewhere. That sentiment grows from an understandable fear that globalization is widening the gap between the haves and the have-nots, threatening local culture and autonomy, and imposing Western values on reluctant societies in the name of universal values.

But Osama bin Laden is neither Lenin nor Marx: he offers neither genuine political leadership nor a constructive alternative vision of the future. If we are to convince the next generation that globalization better serves their self-interest than terrorism, we must contest and defeat bin Laden's arguments in the court of public opinion. Through aggressive public diplomacy, particularly in the Muslim world, we must convince the have-nots that we share their concern about finding better ways to live our common future than in a state of indefinite violence and war. That means we must send our young people overseas not just to fight, but to work with other young people in countries around the world to drain the breeding grounds of anti-Western terror.

In our public diplomacy, we should emphasize that—far from endorsing assaults on Muslim human rights—in recent years, the United States has endured great cost to defend the human rights of Muslims in Kosovo and Bosnia and spoken out against the brutal repression of Chechen Muslims by the Russians and Uighur Muslims by the Chinese in Xinjiang Province. We should publicize the fact that scores of those killed in the World Trade Center were Muslims, the massive human rights abuses committed by the Taliban, and the ways in which the terrorists have distorted the Koran by invoking it to justify human rights abuse. We need to keep working creatively with foreign universities, NGOs, civil society groups, independent media, labor unions, women's groups and political parties to underscore that our universal values coincide with our common interest in ending terrorism. Especially in the Middle East, we must demonstrate to would-be terrorists that terrorism leads nowhere, while the globalization of freedom promotes not just the short-term goal of conflict prevention but also longer-term prosperity and genuine prospects for eventual self-government.

In short, this is first and foremost a test of our commitment to global democracy. The months ahead will test our ability to build as much as our ability to bomb, and challenge our capacity to mobilize the globalization of freedom as the antidote to the globalization of terror.

2.

September 11 was a profound test of our commitment to the rule of law, both abroad and at home. We cannot mistakenly assume that a few terrorist attacks—however brutal—somehow returned us to a state of nature in which there is no law and no rules. In fact, over the centuries, we have developed an elaborate system of domestic and international institutions, regimes, norms, rules, and decision-making procedures precisely to be consulted and obeyed, not ignored, at a time like this.

Both in my work as a lawyer and as a government official, I have learned in crises to ask three questions. First, in framing our response, what does the law *permit?* Second, what does the law *forbid?* And third, which of the available courses of action most closely comports with both the spirit and the letter of the law? If there is such a "law-friendly" course, we should follow it, because doing so will keep the law on our side, keep us on the moral high ground, and preserve the vital support of our allies and international institutions as the crisis proceeds.

In this situation, not surprisingly, international law neither imposes a straitjacket nor gives us a blank check. The September 11 tragedy was a horrible crime, and international law appropriately permits us to mount a forceful response. Article 51 of the United Nations Charter recognizes each member country's "inherent right... of self-defense if an armed attack occurs." In two broad resolutions—the first passed the day after the attack and the second several weeks later—the Security Council clearly authorized UN member states to take action against terrorism, permitting the United States and its allies to use authorized force against both bin Laden and the Taliban who offers him safe haven. In addition, NATO has invoked Article 5 of its charter, which authorizes all member states to use force to respond to an attack from abroad against any NATO member. More fundamentally, the September 11 strikes constituted not just "armed attacks" but crimes against humanity, and if you consider them acts of war, war crimes as well. What all this means is that the United States government enjoys considerable freedom under international law to pursue a broad-based strategy that marshals a forceful military response as part of a larger diplomatic, economic, counterintelligence, and law enforcement strategy.

Given bin Laden's responsibility for the September 11 attacks, international law also permits us to treat him and those in his network as unlawful combatants who can be subjected to a reciprocal and proportionate military response. As our response evolves, we can and should simultaneously follow several tracks to pursue their legal accountability: first, the possibility of trying bin Laden and his accomplices in a United States court (under an indictment that supersedes the one filed against them for the 1993 World Trade Center bombing); second, the option of trying the terrorists in a foreign court, as was done in the Pan Am 103 case (tried in The

Hague under Scottish law); third, considering an international criminal track before an ad hoc international tribunal; and fourth, allowing victims to bring civil lawsuits in U.S. courts against responsible terrorists, their state supporters, and their attachable assets.

But if we choose to treat this as a war, then clearly we must obey the international laws of war. Terrorists scorn the laws of war, but responsible democracies obey them. This means that our military exercises must scrupulously avoid invasions of neutral countries without their consent, the intentional targeting of innocent civilians or civilian targets, and careless strikes on humanitarian facilities. As a rule of thumb, the more massive, the more unilateral, and the more indiscriminate our use of force becomes, the more likely that it will violate international law and alienate the very allies, humanitarian groups, and moderate Muslim states whose support we will need over the long run.

Like international law, U.S. domestic law also leaves the president room for action while counseling restraint. Significantly, in authorizing the president to respond, Congress did *not* declare war, which it has done only five times in our history, and thus did not place us into a legal state of war. Such a declaration would have triggered a series of extraordinary statutory powers that authorize the president in times of declared war to seize property, businesses, and manufacturing facilities, to restrict otherwise lawful political activities, and to obtain wiretaps without a court order.

Nor has Congress declared a formal state of national

emergency, which would have vested additional statutory crisis powers in the president. Instead, seven days after the attack, it announced that the September 11 attacks "pose[d] an unusual and extraordinary threat to the national security and foreign policy of the United States" that warrants giving the president broad statutory authority to respond. Pursuant to that language, Congress overwhelmingly passed a Use of Force Resolution—a statute—that gives the president very broad discretion without time limit to use "all necessary and appropriate force" against all entities—whether foreign or domestic—"so long as he determines that they planned, authorized, committed or aided the September 11 attacks" and so long as his action is "in order to prevent future attacks."

In exercising that discretion, the president is not hand-cuffed by Executive Order No. 12,333. Adopted by President Ford in 1974 and maintained through five successor adminis-trations, that order states that "no person employed or acting on behalf of the United States Government shall engage in, or conspire to engage in assassination." On its face, it was designed to prevent the assassination of foreign leaders, not the killing of foreign terrorists, and has been subsequently construed not to limit "lawful self-defense options." It would be exceedingly bizarre for Osama bin Laden, acting as a combatant, to order the slaughter of nearly 5,000 Americans, then to argue that he cannot be "assassinated" in return because he is an innocent, not a combatant. And even if one were to consider a strike against bin Laden to be an "assassination," the executive order could presumably be repealed, modified, or suspended by the president himself, or deemed overridden by the Use of Force Resolution that became law on September 18.

But to acknowledge that U.S. law gives the president broad discretion to respond does not mean that there are no constraints on his action. Even in war, our Constitution makes clear that the president is our commander-in-chief, not our king. Nor should the Use of Force Resolution be confused with the infamous Gulf of Tonkin Resolution of 1964, which several successive presidents construed as authorizing the escalation of an undeclared war in Vietnam. The ensuing debacle triggered repeal of the Gulf of Tonkin Resolution and the enactment in 1973 of the War Powers Resolution, whose consultation, reporting, and durational limits on presidential warmaking have been U.S. law for nearly thirty years. Far from repealing or superseding the War Powers Resolution, Congress's Use of Force Resolution explicitly invoked that law. This means that as this conflict escalates, the American people, through their elected representatives in Congress, have a legal right to receive reports of U.S. troop commitments abroad, to be consulted, and to authorize the long-term maintenance of United States armed forces in both hostile and imminently hostile situations.

Less than a month after the attacks, after details from a classified intelligence briefing on Capitol Hill were apparently leaked, President Bush briefly overreacted by restricting

top-secret congressional briefings to eight specified congressional leaders. But as the excluded legislators quickly noted,
federal law requires the State Department to keep the House
and Senate foreign affairs committees "fully and currently
informed with respect to all activities and responsibilities
within the jurisdiction of these committees." These statutory
consultation requirements rest on a simple, impeccable logic:
that to conduct a sustained bipartisan foreign policy in time
of crisis, the president should both regularly consult and genuinely listen to elected officials who do not owe their jobs to
him. Korea and Vietnam demonstrated that protracted, open-
ended, undeclared wars tend to leave troops and presidents
unsupported and legislators unaccountable. As with international law, the more the president responds to the unfolding
crisis by regularly consulting with Congress and obeying
domestic statutes, the more likely it is that the rule of law
will remain on his side in the difficult months ahead.

For all of the talk of the struggle ahead as a "war against
terrorism," we should not forget that as a legal matter, we are
neither formally in a state of war nor even in a congression-
ally declared national emergency. Instead, the legal state of
affairs most closely resembles one we experienced at the
founding of the Republic. At that time, pirates, privateers and
other early terrorists posed as great a threat to our nation as
sovereign states bent on war. Article I, section 8, of the U.S.
Constitution, which authorizes Congress to declare war,
elsewhere gave Congress the much narrower power to
"define and punish Piracies, Felonies committed on the High

Seas, and Offenses against the Law of Nations." The framers drafted the language specifically to deal with situations like today's: where private actors—pirates and slave traders—work in tandem with sovereign governments to terrorize the civilized countries of the world. In 1790, Congress exercised this power by passing statutes criminalizing such international crimes as piracy and assaults upon ambassadors. Not long after, Congress supported President Jefferson in authorizing the navy to retaliate against the Barbary pirates. In the past few decades, Congress has again invoked this power to criminalize such "Offenses against the Law of Nations" as attacks against aviation and diplomats, hostage-taking and theft of nuclear materials.

As Congress continues to legislate with regard to the current crisis, it should expressly invoke this specific constitutional power to define the Pentagon and World Trade Center attacks as recognized offenses against the law of nations. Under the Use of Force Resolution, Congress has already authorized the president to use all necessary means to punish the perpetrators. That legislation grants the president discretion to punish terrorists and their supporters by military force or by treating them as international criminals, subject—the way Panama's drug-lord dictator Manuel Noriega was in 1989—to arrest, extradition and trial. By making explicit legislative reference to this constitutional language, Congress would also make clear that American military forces enforcing the Law of Nations are bound to obey the rules of international law—particularly those rules that for-

bid the targeting of innocent civilians or the deliberate inflic-
tion of "collateral damage" upon them.

Clearly, the president must have the option of military
force to eradicate terrorist networks, to hold accountable any
perpetrators who may be captured, and to deter their state
sponsors. But if, as has been widely reported, bin Laden controls up to 10,000 operatives who function in 60 countries,
against how many of these nations do we really want to go to
war? If the president really intends to invoke the constitutional war power, he must do so formally, in consultation and
with the legal authorization of our elected representatives in
Congress. We need not shoehorn the September 11 attacks
into the language of "war" to give our president ample
authority to deal with global terrorists and their state supporters. For under the Law of Nations clause of Article I,
Congress has abundant constitutional power to punish the
perpetrators of the September 11 attacks for what they are:
international criminals and violators of the law of all civilized
nations.

3.

September 11 will also test whether we have genuinely
internalized our universal commitments to respect human
rights, both at home and abroad. Under international law,
this requires us to make every effort to avoid the targeting of
innocent civilians or careless strikes against civilian targets or

humanitarian aid centers. We must not let stray media images of Palestinians celebrating the attacks blind us to the fact that in the repressive societies where we are most likely to strike militarily, such as Afghanistan and Iraq, the innocent civilians are as much victims of human rights abuse as were the thousands who died on September 11. If we respond to this tragedy by killing large numbers of innocent civilians, we will grievously harm our own cause. We will not honor our own civilian dead. We will run afoul of international law. We will lose the moral high ground. We will trigger further cycles of retaliation, and we will surely drive countries out of the global coalition that we must sustain if we are to win this struggle.

Nor can we forget the human rights of the uncounted refugees that armed conflict will surely generate. At this writing, thousands of Afghan refugees are streaming out of Afghanistan into Pakistan to join millions still lingering there after the Soviet conflict of the 1970s and 80s. We must take special pains to ensure that our military action does not endanger humanitarian aid workers on the ground or hamper delivery of emergency food aid that must be distributed now that the snow has begun to fall. As winter sets in and Afghanis cluster in refugee camps or wander in the open, their needs for humanitarian relief and protection will vastly multiply. Left unaddressed, the humanitarian crisis can quickly evolve into a human rights crisis of a magnitude that may dwarf the scope of the original September 11 attacks.

Equally important, we cannot, in the name of payback, diminish our long-standing effort to promote respect for human rights on the part of our coalition partners. Several countries that we have sought to enlist in our antiterrorism campaign—including China, Pakistan, Russia, Saudi Arabia and Uzbekistan—have already signaled their desire for the United States to ignore their domestic human rights abuses as a price for their cooperation. Many countries, particularly in Eastern Europe and Central Asia, have imposed radical restrictions on human rights at home in the name of fighting terrorists. During the cold war, we too often overlooked antidemocratic behavior and human rights abuses by friendly autocrats as the price of enlisting their aid in the war against communism. It would be equally shortsighted and disastrous to our longer-term commitment to promote global democratization if we were now to overlook similar behavior to promote our war against terrorism.

Nor can we diminish or compromise—in the name of war or national emergency—our constitutional commitment to human rights at home. September 11 marked a watershed experience for Americans: the first foreign attack of this magnitude on our mainland in nearly 200 years. In a way that we have not, our fellow democracies like Britain or Israel have had far greater experience than we in balancing a crisis atmosphere, a forceful response, and strenuous efforts to increase homeland security, with a sustained commitment to domestic civil liberties.

Many have called this the second Pearl Harbor. But as an

Asian American whose parents emigrated to the U.S. from South Korea in the 1940s, I cannot forget that the first Pearl Harbor triggered the internment of tens of thousands of loyal Americans based solely on their ethnicity. What few remember is that several noted civil libertarians—President Franklin Delano Roosevelt; Earl Warren, then attorney general of California; Supreme Court Justices Hugo Black and William O. Douglas—not only failed to challenge the Japanese internment, they affirmatively ratified it.

We would repeat grievous errors of history if we once again condoned racial profiling, brutal immigration and employment practices, and unjustified invasions of privacy, all in the name of rooting out terrorists. The history of our civil rights movement has been a struggle to reject invidious discrimination through racial stereotyping. We need to continue that struggle by developing reliable techniques of behavioral profiling that would allow us to detect would-be terrorists based on their conduct and motives, not on their ethnicity.

Unfortunately, these are not simply hypothetical concerns. In response to intense White House pressure, and after radically truncated deliberation, Congress passed—and the president signed—sweeping antiterrorism legislation that would allow the attorney general to detain noncitizens at length as suspected "terrorists" with minimal procedural safeguards. The law allows information obtained during criminal investigations—with respect to U.S. citizens as well as aliens—to be distributed to U.S. intelligence agencies without meaningful limitation on how those agencies can use the obtained information. Moreover, the legislation allows the government to conduct covert searches in furtherance of criminal investigations, for example by entering your home office or other private place to search, take photographs, and download computer files without notifying you until after the fact. Law enforcement officials are permitted to access, use, and disseminate highly personal information in student records about U.S. and foreign students alike. In addition, officials may now use expanded wiretap authority to circumvent the probable cause requirement of the Fourth Amendment, to make chilling invasions of internet privacy, and to eavesdrop without a warrant on conversations of citizens who are not targets of any criminal investigation.

The constitutionality of these laws will no doubt be challenged in court. But the troubling message is that in the first weeks of the crisis, we have not succeeded in avoiding the kind of crisis restrictions that led to the *Pentagon Papers* case or the Alien and Sedition Acts. If we are to ensure that the freedoms of press, travel, communication, religion, and assembly are carefully observed, then all of us—not just the courts and law enforcement officials—must be vigilant to monitor governmental restrictions on rights. The terrorists want to take our freedoms, but they will only succeed if we help them.

4.

Finally, September 11 and its aftermath will test our commitment to an *open society*. Just because our aura of invulnerability has been shattered, we cannot let fear lead us to choke off the openness and mobility that have made us strong.

The first weeks of the crisis have seen a rash of reaction. First, in addition to the antiterrorism bill that rushed through Congress, the president created virtually overnight an Office of Homeland Security. It has been given sweeping but vague powers to coordinate domestic efforts against terrorism, and to "identify priorities and coordinate efforts for collection and analysis of information within the United States regarding... activities of terrorists or terrorist groups within the United States." Second, for the source of the CIA's woes and an implicit cause of the September 11 debacle, several members of Congress have pointed fingers at the Church Committee, the Senate Select Committee, chaired in the late 1970s by the late Senator Frank Church of Idaho, to study government operations with respect to intelligence activities. Third, at the urging of the White House, the television networks agreed not to air unedited videotapes of speeches by bin Laden for fear that they might contain coded messages to his cohorts, and several commentators and comedians have been temporarily banished from the airwaves for comments deemed to be politically incorrect and downright unpatriotic.

Standing alone, none of these reactions seems earthshaking, but taken together, they paint a picture oddly oblivious to recent history. Although the Office of Homeland Security may fill an important bureaucratic gap, its creation also marks an important blurring of a more than fifty-year division of labor between federal domestic law enforcement agencies and international intelligence agencies. In the National Security Act of 1947, Congress expressly denied the CIA police, subpoena, law enforcement and internal security functions to ensure that it would act as a national security agency, not as a domestic law enforcement unit. Yet during the Vietnam War, the CIA blurred that line by conducting illegal secret domestic break-ins, mail intercepts, wiretaps, and domestic surveillance of antiwar activists and domestic protesters. Indeed, we sometimes forget that the infamous Watergate break-in was itself executed by the "plumbers," a White House unit funded with private campaign contributions, partially staffed by former CIA agents, supported by the CIA, and formed for the express purpose of "plugging leaks" by government officials suspected of having exposed the secret bombing of Cambodia. At this writing, how accountable the new OHS will be to Congress or the public remains unclear, given that it is headed by a presidential appointee with cabinet-level status who took office without ever being subjected to congressional confirmation.

Similarly, those who blame the Church Committee for CIA failings forget how that and similar inquiries came about. Following President Nixon's resignation in 1974,

President Ford declared that he would not tolerate illegal activities by the intelligence agencies, and formed the Rockefeller Commission to investigate intelligence abuse, followed by the creation of the Church and other committees to oversee government intelligence operations. In the late 1970s, those committees offered a comprehensive 263-page charter for reform of the intelligence community. But after extensive debate, legislative opponents trimmed that bill down into the two-page Intelligence Oversight Act of 1980, which ended up making only a few modest revisions in the law.

The Soviet invasion of Afghanistan and the fall of the Shah of Iran, both deemed intelligence failures, further dampened public concern over CIA misconduct. During the Reagan administration, however, a team of White House staff members charged with supporting the covert war in Central America was discovered illegally selling arms to Iran and diverting the proceeds to the contras, the Nicaraguan resistance. After the Iran-Contra Affair, Congress again established House and Senate committees to study intelligence abuses and proposed new amendments to the Intelligence Oversight Act.

These were ultimately shelved after President Reagan left office, so as not to unduly tie the hands of the new president, George H.W. Bush. Thus, even after the Church Committee's report, successive scandals regarding intelligence misconduct have proceeded from revelation to public outrage to blue-ribbon investigation to legislative reform proposals, which have been largely retracted in deference to executive pledges of good faith that later proved seriously ineffective to forestall future abuse.

Third and finally, the growing insistence on "patriotic correctness" is disturbingly reminiscent of both World War II and the cold war McCarthy era. We must be troubled when the networks self-censor not just hostile messages but also harmless speech on the grounds that they are unpatriotic or politically incorrect. In the months ahead, we need to speak out forthrightly, even when the message is unwelcome. We must tell the truth about human rights violations, whether committed by the terrorists or by our coalition partners; Israelis or Palestinians; the Pakistanis, the Taliban, or the Northern Alliance; or even our own government officials. Our courts, legislators, and law enforcement officials must meticulously respect our freedoms to speak, write, travel, worship and assemble, and give special protection to those who would protest against government policies.

But it will not be enough for us simply to defend our freedoms. We have to *use* those freedoms. As our government is called on to do more, and as we as citizens are called on to do more, disagreement will inevitably arise about both the appropriate means and ends of government policy. As a society, we need to beware the oppressive orthodoxy of "appropriate patriotism." To foster robust debate, we must speak out strongly against the notion that it is somehow inappropriate to question what our government chooses to do. It is never unpatriotic to question what our government does in our name, especially in time of war.

Our enemies in this war are out to destroy our society precisely because it is open, tolerant, pluralistic and democratic. In its place, they seek to promote one that is closed, vengeful, repressive and absolutist. To secure genuine victory, we must make sure that they fail, not just in their assault on our safety but also in their challenge to our most fundamental values.

CHAPTER 7

RETHINKING THE UNTHINKABLE: NEW PRIORITIES FOR NEW NATIONAL SECURITY

Paul Bracken

I N   T H E   I M M E D I A T E   aftermath of the attacks on September 11, the U.S. government was primed to shoot down an American passenger jet if it appeared to be heading toward the White House or the Capitol. Endorsing this dreadful option, Senator Hillary Clinton said, "In desperate times like these, you have to think the unthinkable. And I, for one, would not have second-guessed that decision."

Since then, the term unthinkable has been widely used to describe both what happened on September 11 and what many feared might happen next. The word had been part of the vocabulary of the atomic age, ever since the strategist Herman Kahn wrote *Thinking About the Unthinkable* in 1962. But there was a big difference between the two uses of the term—the one applied to September 11 and the one used during the cold war. Kahn, in his lectures and writings, always emphasized that he wasn't actually thinking the unthinkable—he was only thinking about the unthinkable. Senator Clinton dropped the preposition. Now there was no "about" about it: foreign forces had delivered a devastating blow against American citizens on American soil.

The September 11 attack was unexpected and brazen, like Pearl Harbor, but it was unique in several ways. Though the perpetrators were quickly identified, they didn't actually take credit.

Also, it was an unprecedented attempt to ignite a war between civilizations. Osama bin Laden said as much in his television interview on October 7. That feature of the threat conjured up in American minds a sense of a threat coming from many directions. In the weeks that followed, citizens had to contend not just with the danger that planes would fall from the sky and giant buildings would tumble down, but that day-to-day activities as mundane as opening their mail could be fatal.

In addition to its jarring, even transforming effect on national life, September 11 marked a watershed in our understanding of what it takes to ensure the stability of the international system—and what it takes for our enemies to upset that stability. Traditionally, war had been seen as an activity in which states engaged against each other. While renegade individuals could always make their dent on history—an assassin on a street corner in Sarajevo in 1914, for example—large-scale violence of the kind that could shake a world power to its core was always seen as a monopoly of the nation-state. Moreover, major international conflict had been on the wane in recent years. Saddam Hussein was the last head of state to try a full-scale invasion of a neighboring country—an activity that had been commonplace through history. Saddam had been repulsed by a U.S.-led coalition on behalf of something called "the international community," what many believed to be an increasingly coherent assembly of states that was united by certain interests and values and that could enforce its will on miscreants. That a small group of terrorists armed with box cutters and a martyr complex could do so much damage showed the fragility of that construct. Bin Laden threatened not just the safety of the U.S. but the very idea that there *is* a single international community, not to mention one that is capable of deterring this whole new kind of war.

I.

September 11 began with a failure of intelligence. The nation was not warned of the attack, nor was it prepared when it came. Regardless of what happens in any military action, improvements in intelligence and homeland defense will be part of the new definition of American security.

A wide variety of rationalizations can be used to explain why the attacks of September 11 were such a surprise. Inadequate human intelligence, a political failure to act on the intelligence that was provided, and the sheer impossibili-

ty of reliably forecasting a surprise attack are the most frequently offered explanations. Each has something to it.

But rationalizations do not prevent future surprises.
Unless the U.S. improves its intelligence system there will be
far less payoff from improving other areas of defense because
the consequences of inadequate intelligence are so enormous. No amount of improved homeland defense can com-
pensate for poor intelligence. Imagine what the cold war
would have been like had the U.S. lacked good intelligence.
Our nuclear forces would have had to be placed on hair-trigger alert, sharply increasing the danger of accidental atomic
war. Our armies in Europe would have been much larger to
prepare for a surprise attack because there would not have
been time to reinforce them. The crises in the 1960s in Cuba
and Berlin would have been much more likely to tip into
war—a danger that was avoided largely because of intelligence. Good intelligence was directly responsible for the stability of the cold war competition. Its importance in the war
against terrorism will be just as important.

For several years the CIA, the National Security Agency,
which conducts surveillance around the world, and other
parts of the intelligence community have been improving in
a number of areas, and programs were under way before
September 11 for further progress in correcting deficiencies.
Though problems remain, it would be a big mistake to gut
the existing intelligence system in a hasty effort to start over
with a new one. Experience in a wide range of organizational reforms, in business and government, shows that top-to-

bottom upheavals in the name of reform almost always lower overall performance of the affected organization.

Contrary to popular belief, large organizations can be turned around quickly without tearing them apart. Changes at America's leading businesses in the 1990s—at IBM, GE, and Allied Signal—are examples of how leadership identified existing core competencies and built new ones. That is the challenge for the intelligence community now.

Broadly speaking, the current system is good at technical intelligence, especially finding out things like how many missiles China has pointed at Taiwan. But improvement is needed in a number of areas. One problem is that many new technical systems have only recently been added, and we lack the operating experience to use them effectively. Unmanned airplanes that carry missiles, cameras and "ears" are an example. They are brand new and it takes time to work out all of the bugs.

Another big problem is that radio signals used to be picked up by antennas. These, plus photographs from satellites and airplanes, gave us most of our intelligence. In the information age this has changed radically. Today signals are digitized—broken down into zeros and ones—to suit the language of computers. Digital information is sent over the Internet and through fiber-optic lines (both undersea and underground), and over cellular telephones that bypass the traditional phone network. It is much harder to collect this kind of information. When encrypted it is harder still.

What is required here is a national effort on the scale of what happened when satellite photography first became pos-

sible in the 1950s. The CIA drew on the best minds in corporate America to understand that technology. There has already
been a great deal of effort put into the new information technologies by the intelligence community. More resources are
definitely needed, but the overall direction of this program is
understood and well under way. This is one more example of
why the intelligence community should not be turned upside
down by imprudent overhauls. The likely effect would only
be to disrupt improvements already happening.

New competencies for an age of terror are where intelligence change is most needed. The best way to defeat terrorists is to penetrate their cells. But to do this requires skills that
have fallen off in the intelligence community over several
decades. The CIA needs better human intelligence: the ability to develop foreign agents, get inside information from
those who know about terrorism, and be in a position to
understand the terrorists' mindset to anticipate their next
moves. Agents are needed who possess the language and
expertise to get inside these organizations.

The prospects for rapid improvement here are not good.
The problem isn't one of loosening rules about working
with unsavory individuals, or prohibitions against assassination of foreign leaders. The problems go much deeper than
this, and any attempt at a quick fix—by changing these regulations—will at best create an illusion of change and at worst
involve the U.S. in actions it will regret.

The CIA once had a superb human intelligence system. In
the late 1940s it organized the dockworkers in France and

the Italian labor unions against communism. These actions were every bit as important as NATO armies in preserving Western Europe's security. Had France or Italy fallen to the communists through general strikes or even rigged elections, it would have given communism the momentum of appearing to be the wave of the future.

What needs to happen to fight terrorism is to re-create this level of human talent, but to focus it on the Middle East, Asia, and elsewhere, and adapt it to the modern needs of countering terrorism.

The early CIA was made up of worldly people in the best sense of the term. U.S. intelligence operatives knew the leaders of their countries. Agents came from a socioeconomic background that put them in the elite circles of business and finance. They had personal connections that could put them in touch with people throughout the societies of foreign countries, high and low.

At the same time, President Eisenhower poured money into American universities to provide the nation with well-trained area experts who had the language training and background to understand their regions of expertise. The 1958 National Defense Education Act funded Russian language training for a generation of scholars, diplomats and spies. Contrast this with the immediate aftermath of September 11, the spectacle of government trying to recruit people capable of speaking Pushtu, the language spoken by the members of the Taliban. It is astonishing that ten years after the end of the cold war, there has still been no comparable effort by the government to revitalize language and area studies at American universities.

The political situation today is, of course, much different than in the 1950s. After the Vietnam War many universities wanted little or nothing to do with the government in areas such as this. In the 1990s, top students sought careers in investment banking, not the CIA. But America has one of the most globalized economies. Its businesses are everywhere. Therefore, there is a rich set of resources and people to draw on to support an expanded human intelligence program. Programs for lateral career entry, greater cooperation with the private sector, and information exchanges that meet the needs of all those involved are needed.

This is a long-term problem. Trying to fix it in the short term simply with looser regulations on what the CIA can do in the back alleys and badlands of the world will only divert attention from what is really needed—a ten-year effort to greatly expand the language and area knowledge for the country as a whole, from which the CIA can draw.

Closer relations between the CIA and universities are essential, for in today's world no single organization can acquire the knowledge needed about the world. It would be an enormous mistake to set up language and area studies institutions within the government to do this. Such a move would only reinforce insular attitudes, and their competency could never match what America's great universities could offer.

Finally, the distinction made between human and technical intelligence needs to be fundamentally reconsidered. This is a big difference from the 1950s. Success comes from the two together, not from relying on one over the other.

According to press reports, the earliest sign that the attacks of September 11 were coming came from an intercepted phone call from Osama bin Laden telling his wife in Syria to return to Afghanistan. Had there been a CIA agent in bin Laden's cell, this important information could have been used to order him to immediately begin some disruptions to forestall attack. An agent might also have been able to tell CIA headquarters which bogus internet messages to plant that would set off dissension in the group. To do this requires human and technical intelligence, working together.

The principle here is one that has worked well in business. What has revolutionized management in the past ten years is the integration of new technologies with human talents. It is not a question of one or the other.

The intelligence problem is fixable. The key is to not tear apart the competencies we already have. The bigger challenge is to create the new ones in effective ways. We need a new generation of intelligence professionals who understand how to operate human agents and the technical systems in a seamless way.

2.

The second conspicuous failure of September 11 was in homeland defense. The fact that the Pentagon itself was on the terrorists' target list—and, more to the point, that it was successfully hit—is proof that the Department of Defense is, in a very real sense, misnamed. In the decade after the cold war, it could have been called at various times the Department of Regional Stability, or Peacekeeping, or Containment of Rogue States, or even what it had been called up until 1947— the Department of War. The term and concept of defense were stretched to absurd lengths. Interventions in Somalia and the Balkans, environmental security, and economic security were all included. The only thing left out was the defense of the American people. While the U.S. was going forth into the world to slay, or at least tame, dragons like Saddam Hussein and Slobodan Milosevic, a vulnerability was lurking here at home that few wished to acknowledge.

The U.S. was vulnerable in at least two ways on September 11: from the airplane attacks on the World Trade Center and the Pentagon and from the anthrax campaign that soon followed it. Those experiences suggested other vulnerabilities—to contamination of our water supply, to attacks on other parts of our infrastructure and, the ultimate nightmare scenario, to weapons of mass destruction. What most shocked Americans was the ease with which the four airplanes were hijacked. The hijackers were trained in U.S. flying schools, traveled around the country under their own names and were in frequent communication with one another. No one noticed—or at least, no one did anything about it. In the weeks that followed, most government officials still couldn't pronounce the terrorists' names properly.

The bioterrorist incidents that followed looked like a Keystone Cops movie. Anthrax cases went unreported. Technicians in New York accidentally contaminated part of the laboratory for testing the presence of anthrax, slowing down the diagnosis. Florida officials told workers at a newspaper office that it was safe to work there, even though a photo editor had died of anthrax, then shut the office down after much of the staff had worked there through the weekend. One house of Congress closed while the other stayed open. We learned that no one had stockpiled adequate supplies of antibiotics and vaccines. And throughout it all the government told the public not to panic.

This slapdash response underscores the need for an overhaul of homeland security. Following the attacks of September 11, America's first Office of Homeland Security was established. In the U.S., those responsible for this function are scattered across forty federal agencies, including the Coast Guard, parts of the CIA, parts of the military, the Centers for Disease Control, Border Control, the FBI, the Secret Service and at least two dozen other entities. But looking at homeland defense as a problem of organizational fragmentation is a mistake because it suggests that there is an organizational fix. The problems of homeland security cut across so many sectors—computer networks, commercial airlines, the tracking of dangerous individuals, the protection of our ports—that it is virtually impossible to consolidate authority into any single agency.

The U.S. is now in the "get started" stage of homeland

defense. The basics need to be emphasized: protecting our borders, stockpiling vaccines and antibiotics in case of biological attack, monitoring ship and air traffic, and better surveillance technology. The problem is of such urgency that there should not be too much concern over wasting money, at least in the short term.

That said, the new Office of Homeland Security will have to decide which of these programs makes sense for the long term. Responsibility for monitoring the spread of biological agents should stay with the Centers for Disease Control. Port protection should stay with the Coast Guard. Air marshals should protect our airplanes. It makes no sense for a new agency to try to control these programs day to day.

What does make sense is for the Office of Homeland Security to make the trade-offs between different programs. Unless those are understood and put before the president for decision in an orderly and timely fashion, the government will fly off in all directions. Which is better: tougher border controls or national identity cards? Border control means perimeter defense—stopping bad guys before they come in—while a system of national ID cards might help with defense in depth—catching them when they're already here. Helping the president make those judgments should be one of the major roles of the Office of Homeland Security.

Another role for the office is to think through emergency plans so that, if activated, at least they don't make the problem worse. A study by Los Alamos National Laboratory found that traffic jams after a bioterror incident would unintentionally funnel thousands of people downwind of the attack, greatly increasing casualties. In this case, the transportation system was an unwitting accomplice in mass murder. What government official could possibly have thought of this in the middle of a crisis? If the issues are understood before a crisis, then plans can be made to respond much better than we did after September 11.

The challenge for homeland defense in the short term is to spend whatever it takes to play catch-up—to think through the scenarios and make the preparations that were shown to be woefully lacking on September 11. In the long term, it is to decide what programs make sense in light of complex and poorly understood interrelationships.

3.

The political consequences of America being a terrorist battleground also need greater attention. In the past our intense crises have been far away. It was several years after the initial American intervention in Vietnam before the issue took hold in the U.S. That happened once American soldiers started coming home in body bags.

Now we've seen body bags on the streets of New York. America is in the terror zone; the home front is the battleground. As a result, the relative freedom we enjoyed for so long to decide on a national course of action without considering its immediate impact at home is gone. In many ways this is a complicating factor. It means that leaders will have a harder time controlling the pace of a crisis or a war. Controlling the tempo of a crisis is often critical to its resolution. It takes time to sort out the facts of what has actually happened. And because most of America's military power is at home the Pentagon needs time to move abroad. The luxury of considered action may be one of the biggest casualties of September 11.

As a society, we will have to learn to live with terrorism. It is in that sense, more than any other, that people are right when they say that everything has changed. This leads to a paradoxical situation. Overnight, living with the threat of terrorism became part of everyday life. Disagreeable as that reality is, it's better than the alternative of lulling ourselves into false complacency, sloppy protection and haphazard responses.

Israel and other countries have had to live with terror for a long time. That means striking a balance. A society coping with terrorism can't react in a spasmodic or chaotic way to each incident, forgetting what it learned from the last one; nor can it stay on hyperalert for years. Helping us to strike that balance is another task under the heading of homeland security.

There is, or should be, a critical linkage between the way we protect our people at home and the way we hit our enemies abroad. If an American city is threatened or struck with a chemical or biological attack, the president will need to have the ability to evacuate the city quickly and also the option of striking fast against foreign targets. The evacuation itself will help legitimize the strikes, and the reprisals, if delivered promptly, may damage the terrorists' ability to carry out a follow-up attack. All this requires pre-designation of targets and pre-positioning of planes and other military assets to conduct the strikes. The Israelis have been doing this kind of thing for years. It's part of their national security culture. It may have to become part of ours.

4.

September 11 underscored what should be a new priority for American diplomacy: the effort to slow down the proliferation of dangerous technology.

After the collapse of the Soviet Union and the end of the cold war, the great hope was that the world would develop in benign ways, focusing on economic development and political liberalization. There was significant progress in that direction. But there have also been some disturbing trends, particularly the growth of the nuclear weapons club to include India and Pakistan, with a number of other countries knocking on the door. Along a wide belt stretching halfway around the globe, from Israel to North Korea, a number of nations either have acquired or are bent on acquiring weapons of mass destruction and the capability of launching them with ballistic missiles.

The U.S.-Soviet nuclear standoff was perilous enough at moments of crisis, given the possibility of hair-trigger miscalculations, accidental launch or some "mad major" pressing the button on his own authority. In the second nuclear age that is now upon us, those risks are far greater, given the multiplicity of animosities and the absence of either the habits or the systems for averting conflict.

Of all the permutations and combinations, the India–Pakistan matchup is the most worrisome, since those two countries have declared and demonstrated their nuclear capability and have already fought four wars, including a severe and prolonged skirmish in 1999. Mutual deterrence, escalation control, crisis management and other concepts developed between the U.S. and the Soviet Union during the cold war simply aren't part of the vocabulary, mindset or behavior patterns in the Middle East and South Asia. It is all too easy to imagine a crisis that might begin with an incident of terrorism—say, another massacre in Kashmir of the kind that has been common in recent years, followed by an Indian retaliation of some kind—that spins out of control.

Against that backdrop, India and Pakistan should have an incentive to get serious about regulating their arms race. The U.S. is uniquely positioned to help them do so.

5.

Aside from their nuclear competition, India and Pakistan have used terrorism as a covert extension of their foreign and defense policies (though Pakistan has relied more on terror than India). There was no comparable danger in the air between the U.S. and the Soviet Union during the cold war. The nuclear balance between the superpowers remained stable largely because they exercised self-restraint in the way they conducted their global and regional rivalries. Although there were a few exceptions, such as East Germany's support for the Red Army faction in West Germany, neither the Soviets nor their Warsaw Pact allies relied much on terrorism in their effort to subvert the U.S. and its interests.

Precisely because the U.S. has good relations with both India and Pakistan, it has unique leverage to get them to stop sending infiltrators armed with explosives across each other's borders and to stop supporting indigenous violent groups on each other's territory. The arguments for doing so are compelling—indeed, irrefutable. The vicious cycle of provocation and reprisal is hard to control. So, for that matter, are the terrorist groups that one side or the other might think they're using as pawns. Terrorists are, by definition, resistant to authority and contemptuous of traditional political, not to mention diplomatic, considerations and constraints. They defy their bankrollers and their hosts, just as they defy the rest of the world. They are the original Frankenstein monsters. Just ask the Saudis.

So American officials start with some traction in the tough talks that lie ahead with their counterparts in New Delhi and Islamabad.

The bigger problem is what to do about the rogue states, particularly Iraq. September 11 and its aftermath, particularly the ominous arrival of anthrax on the scene, emphasize that we are dealing with terrorists who, even though they are pursuing their own goals and taking orders from no one, apparently have some sort of help from states that have invested years of effort into acquiring the technology of mass murder. These are states that have climbed the technology ladder and are now able to lob weapons at us that are as sophisticated as they are lethal. Some of those states—again, Iraq is Exhibit A—will be only too willing to turn over this knowledge to terrorists. Whether they train their own agents or simply spread what they have learned to groups whose goals advance those of Saddam Hussein and his ilk, the prospects are daunting.

Milling anthrax spores so that they can penetrate the human lung, preparing the proper mixture of sarin gas or mounting a plan to infect a city with a few suicide carriers of smallpox—these are among the "core competencies" of modern terrorism. They used to be the monopoly of the U.S. and the Soviet Union. Now they have spread to some twenty-five nations; and, from there, we must assume, they have gotten into the hands of terrorist groups around the world. Technology transfer from the nation-state to the terrorist means that even untrained individuals now can cause spectacular levels of damage and carnage.

In this menace—now so dramatically brought home to the entire world—lies an opportunity. If the international community is going to survive as a working concept, it must prove itself up to the task of *unanimous* support for prohibitions on dangerous exports and severe, sustained punishment of any states that violate those prohibitions. Indeed, the term "rogue" should acquire universally accepted meaning with respect to any state that engages in the kind of activity that puts anthrax or sarin or smallpox into the arsenal of groups like al Qaeda. That would mean, in the case of Iraq, that all other countries—whatever their sympathies or special interests—would join in isolating the current Baghdad regime or any other that trafficked in biological, chemical or nuclear weaponry.

By the same token, the current crisis enhances America's ability to lead this effort in the United Nations and elsewhere. As the aggrieved party in the terror campaign that began on September 11, the U.S. starts with an advantage in the coming rounds of deliberation and debate over how to tighten existing controls, formulate new ones and—even more important—enforce *all* controls.

Bin Laden, his minions and his backers intended for the revulsion and fear they inspired to divide the world. It would be fitting (though insufficient) punishment for them if, instead, the effect of what they did were to bring the world together in putting an end to the worst of all bad businesses: the proliferation of weapons of mass destruction.

CHAPTER 8

THE CHALLENGE
TO SCIENCE:
HOW TO MOBILIZE
AMERICAN INGENUITY

Maxine Singer

"THE METHODS AND mechanisms of warfare have altered radically in recent times and they will alter still further in the future. The country is singularly fitted, by reason of the ingenuity of its people, the knowledge and skill of its scientists, the flexibility of its industrial structure, to excel in the arts of peace, and to excel in the arts of war if that be necessary. The scientists and engineers of the country... in close collaboration with the armed services, can be of substantial aid in the task which lies before us."

These words, written by Vannevar Bush in June 1940, are as pertinent to the challenge we face after September 11 as they were a year and a half before Pearl Harbor brought the U.S. into World War II. Bush, a bold engineer and "irrepressible inventor," had moved to Washington from MIT in the late thirties to preside over research at the Carnegie Institution of Washington—the job that I hold today.

President Franklin D. Roosevelt and Bush agreed that the U.S. would soon be at war and that science would be critical to victory. Roosevelt scrawled an "okay" and his initials on what Bush had written and gave him the money and authority to establish the National Defense Research Committee (NDRC) under Bush's leadership. This was an end run around the War Department and the military services. Bush believed that the bureaucracy, secrecy, and rivalries within the military establishment walled it off from access to the most innovative scientific and technical ideas. It was a two-way street blocked in both directions. The military could not, or would not, engage the most inventive and original minds from the private sector, and the private sector had no route to reach the military. Moreover, Bush believed that the lack of full communication and cooperation between the branches of the military itself further diminished their ability to respond to war.

Money was promptly made available from the White House emergency funds and the NDRC started work. In May 1941, the NDRC and the newly formed Committee on Medical Research were combined into an Office of Scientific Research and Development (OSRD) and funding was thereafter provided by Congress. By then, important projects were under way, overseen by Bush and the group of distinguished scientists who formed the governing committee.

By the end of World War II, the OSRD had enlisted and supported thousands of scientists, physicians, and engineers nationwide to apply their originality and skills to a new kind of warfare. Radar, the atomic bomb, the proximity fuse, and penicillin were among the OSRD's novel contributions to the Allied victories.

The OSRD's challenge was threefold. It had to identify problems that needed attention, match them to inventive, competent scientists and engineers nationwide, and put them promptly to work with sufficient support. It needed to convince the military that the ideas and devices produced outside the government were worth learning about and applying to the problems of waging war and eventually ensuring peace. The military had its own scientists and scientific programs, but as Daniel Kevles, the distinguished historian of science, has noted, "There was simply no overarching organization within the military establishment designed to link the technical bureaus of the two services [army and navy] with each other or the civilian world." Finally, the OSRD needed to organize the efficient production of devices and oversee their use in the field so that they could be constantly improved.

Clearing the way for innovative, useful, collaborative research was not easy. Bush schemed incessantly against those sectors of the military establishment that were most resistant to cooperation with civilians and with one another. He made it clear that the OSRD's job was to provide ideas and research not, at least at the start, to take over the development of weaponry or the tactical and strategic responsibilities of the armed forces. Eventually, he succeeded in fostering joint efforts between the military scientists and engineers and those whom the OSRD mustered from the universities and industry.

I.

When, on September 11, the U.S. found itself plunged into a new kind of war, against vicious global terrorism, the challenge was different from the one we'd faced in the 1940s, but now, as then, the nation needs the special talents of its scientists and engineers.

In World War II, the aggressors were clearly identified. The nature of the weapons and Axis offensives were largely predictable, although new technology was anticipated. The U.S. entered the war late after a period of near isolation. While civilian populations around the world were targets of severe attacks, U.S. civilians and territory were, except for Pearl Harbor, never threatened and, at least for us, the war, though all-consuming, was the business of the military.

Today's terrorist aggression is also global, but the perpetrators, their headquarters, their weapons, and the nature, timing and targets of their attacks are unpredictable, as we have learned to our great sorrow. Whatever comes next will probably be, like what came before, clever, cheap, simple, and deadly. The U.S. has not been isolationist since the end of World War II and has exercised its military, diplomatic, economic and technical power worldwide for half a century. The underside of global reach and global engagement is homeland vulnerability.

By the late 1930s, the U.S. military considered technical research essential but economic and political considerations kept expenditures at only 0.6 percent of the War Department's budget. More importantly, the effort was not innovative; the most that could be said, according to Kevles, was that it "had at least brought the devices of World War I to a state of greater sophistication and effectiveness."

Today, competent scientists and engineers are part and parcel of the efforts of the Department of Defense, the Central Intelligence Agency, the National Security Agency and the Federal Bureau of Investigation. Together, these agencies have a bewildering array of programs designed to connect them to new knowledge and technologies, It is, however, unclear whether that knowledge is effectively shared by different programs within any agency. The situation appears to be worse when it comes to interagency connections with the science agencies, such as the National Institutes of Health (NIH), the National Science Foundation (NSF) and the National Aeronautics and Space Administration (NASA). As in the late 1930s, scientists familiar with the situation worry about the robustness of the agencies' connections with new research and how rapidly and intelligently it is being applied. Moreover, though some attention has been paid to defense against terrorist attacks and counterterrorism, purely military matters dominate.

Since the end of the cold war and in spite of the increasing worries about terrorism, the Defense Department budget for research and development has decreased by about a third. The situation in the intelligence agencies is more worrisome than in the Pentagon, even though intelligence is an essential weapon against terrorism. Informed estimates suggest that only 2 to 3 percent of the CIA's operating budget, a total of about $80 million is spent on research and development.

The agencies do reach out to some extent for scientific and technical advice from the private sector. However, there is concern among the scholars, scientists and engineers who work in our great universities, industries, and research institutions that the government agencies are not readily open to the novel understandings and original ideas that could generate much more than just new ways of using existing technology. Many researchers are trained and experienced problem solvers whose approach to difficult problems is to use their expertise to discern obscure patterns and analyze them by stepping "out of the box." This includes scholars with profound insights into the nations that produce or harbor terrorists. Our fight against international terrorism will require their attention and ideas if it is to succeed.

As in Vannevar Bush's day, professionals, including those in the military, regardless of how skilled and dedicated, tend to approach new challenges with old methods and mindsets. This is not a criticism—it is simply the way most of us function. With every good intention, the U.S. military and intelligence agencies will be hampered if they ignore the knowledge and ideas outside the government. This thought was behind the establishment of the Defense Advanced Research Projects Agency (DARPA) by the Pentagon in 1958. Originally, the structure of DARPA was modeled on Vannevar Bush's OSRD, and its operational approach emulated the broad goals typical of OSRD. This meant that individuals with smart ideas were encouraged to bring them forward for support. Over nearly a half century, DARPA has gone through a variety of organizational and programmatic changes. It has given up its earlier broadly defined goals in exchange for more specific projects defined by the military establishment. Consequently, it is much less likely to obtain unusual ideas from the external community, ideas that speak not only to a perceived goal in new ways, but to unimagined goals. Also, though the earlier DARPA could respond promptly to good ideas (during the cold war it could grant funds in a couple of hours if presented with a good idea that fit its broad goals), it now has a lengthy process involving extensive review of proposals prior to making funds available. There is, of course, much benefit to obtaining careful evaluation of proposals, but there is also a substantial price in time lost during a crisis situation. Further delays occur because researchers have problems discovering where in the bureaucracy they should go to take the next steps with successful DARPA-sponsored research.

DARPA is supporting some important and innovative research. Inventive, even futuristic programs were presented in testimony to Congress in June 2001. However, according to that same testimony, only 15 percent of DARPA's budget is devoted to issues relevant for homeland security and defense, such as biological and information warfare. And the primary focus is protection of military forces. However, authoritative advice from independent organizations—such as the National Academies (of Science, Engineering, and Medicine) and the RAND Corporation—has long urged an independent focus on civilian populations. The military's strategies for dealing with chemical and biological weapons on the battlefield are not likely to be readily adaptable for use by civilian health providers.

2.

Confronting terrorist threats at home requires radical rethinking by those accustomed to operating with disciplined and trained personnel in battlefield situations. Will the military and intelligence agencies be better able to restructure their thinking than when Vannevar Bush struggled to persuade the navy to use airplanes equipped with radar against German submarines or the army to try the amphibious trucks? The chief of naval operations, who believed that traditional convoys were the best way to protect allied shipping against German U-boats in the North Atlantic, resisted using newly developed airborne radar to locate and track the submarines and direct destroyers to the prey. Early in the war, 40 allied ships were sunk in the Atlantic for every U-boat destroyed. When the new system went into effect, the ratio quickly dropped to less than one to one and the Germans withdrew the U-boats. This was only one of the accomplishments of the "brilliant and eccentric" scientists at the OSRD's so-called Rad Lab. As for the amphibious trucks, Army Ordinance, responsible for designing and building trucks, rejected it out of hand; according to Bush "they knew all about the subject and they did not want any bright boys playing in their backyard." Eventually, the army changed its mind and the amphibious trucks were vital to successful landings in the Pacific, North Africa, Sicily, and the Normandy beaches on D-day.

The academic community itself does not always make collaboration with defense and intelligence agencies easy. It has habits that can discourage its members from contributing to national needs. Scholars treasure their customary independence and can be loath to concentrate on particular tasks or meet schedules and milestones as industrial scientists do. Using patriotism and the carrot of research support, the OSRD successfully imposed strict project management.

The knottiest challenge, however, will be establishing the essential coordination and communication between researchers and federal, state, and local agencies concerned with homeland security. Knowledgeable people say that agency representatives talk a good game about sharing and cooperation at meetings, but revert to protecting their turf when the meetings are over. We have already experienced conflicting scientific information from people in the national government and between local and national officials. There are already signs that various agencies will recruit their own stables of researchers and impose on them confidentiality rules. The public can rightfully ask, Who is in charge? The situation calls for strong leadership in an era when an autocratic style like Vannevar Bush's is no longer feasible.

The military and intelligence communities tend to believe that secrecy is always the most desirable option. In contrast, academic science traditionally opposes secrecy not least because open publication is its customary output and source of evaluation. Free, international scientific exchange is the norm and has been greatly facilitated by the internet. However, strict confidentiality has always operated in industrial research and the growing interactions between university researchers and biotechnology and information technology companies have made secret work more acceptable. Vannevar Bush surprised the military by dealing strictly and successfully with the requirement for secrecy. Bush was, however, frustrated by the amount of time it took the FBI to provide the necessary security clearances. For him, every minute lost was precious. Today, it takes months for the FBI to clear presidential nominees for government posts even when no crisis looms.

Secrecy is, of course, often essential for intelligence work and for military planning. However, the considerations are different when homeland security and defense are at issue. There is a tremendous advantage to a well-informed public when the risks are biological or chemical attacks. The thousands of local officials responsible for public health and safety must be prepared to deal with emergencies on site. Recently, both the Environmental Protection Agency and the Centers for Disease Control and Prevention removed from their public websites certain information about dangerous chemicals, their locations nationwide, and plans for handling emergencies involving those materials. Officials at chemical plants readily followed suit. Everyone argued that secrecy was necessary to keep the information from would-be terrorists. But the chemical companies, which had for years disliked having to inform local people about the hazards in their neighborhoods, likely welcomed the opportunity. And, in October, Health and Human Services Secretary Tommy G. Thompson defended the website cleanups by trying to reassure everyone that the government was "prepared to take care of any contingency, any consequence that develops for any kind of bioterrorism attack," and adding, "I want to calm the American people."

But trust in Washington may not be very helpful at dispersed, hazardous targets. Communities and local emergency officials in the vicinity of such sites are now less well informed and therefore both unable to press for improved safety and less than fully prepared to deal with and report on accidental or intentional release of nasty stuff. As a general matter, Americans are pragmatic and deal well with frightening facts, they don't need to be coddled. They are much less likely to panic if they know what is going on.

The tendency toward secrecy needs constant surveillance from Congress and the public. A serious balancing of the risks and benefits of secrecy and openness should be part of all decisions regarding keeping information from the public.

3.

The main concerns of the OSRD's medical arm, the Committee on Medical Research, were the health of the armed forces and treatment of the wounded. Its achievements, including improved protection against and treatment for malaria and the development and production of penicillin, the first antibiotic, had tremendous payoffs for civilians after the war. Now, our worries are about the deliberate introduction of diseases and nasty chemical agents into civilian populations. And threats directed at water supplies or the production of animal, plant, and marine food are as serious as those aimed at people. Moreover, many of the possible threats can also have profound effects on our already stressed natural environment.

President Richard Nixon renounced the development and use of biological weapons as a matter of U.S. policy. The 1995 Biological Weapons Convention and the 1993 Chemical Weapons Convention, as imperfect as they are, declare that the use of such agents by states for hostile purposes is outside of international norms. Whatever comfort these policies offered has disappeared with the appearance of an uncivilized and lawless enemy, but they do remain important precepts for international cohesiveness in the face of terror.

The means the terrorists used to wreak destruction and commit mass murder at the World Trade Center and Pentagon came as a complete surprise. In contrast, there has been a great deal of serious analysis of the threat of biological and chemical terrorism. Searching the web for the word bioterrorism yields a lot of authoritative information. Likely agents have been identified and their properties described, including anthrax, botulinin toxin, and smallpox among biological agents and common nasty chemicals such as chlorine, mustard gas, and sarin. War "games" have been played and real events such as the sarin gas attacks by the Japanese Aum Shinrikyo cult have helped shape thoughtful civil defense plans. We could have been prepared but in spite of all this available knowledge, we are not.

The anthrax attack generated misinformation, rampant anxiety, and erroneous and varied statements from public officials and the media. We failed to take advantage of extensive, public information. In the past, there always seemed to be more pressing needs than terrorism for the attention and funds available to responsible officials in local, state, and federal governments. The GAO reports that, including research, the federal government spent only about $350 million on preparation for bioterrorism in the last fiscal year. The Senate has now proposed increasing this fivefold and giving more than a third of the funds to state and local efforts where it belongs. Even if bioterrorism never went beyond the present anthrax situation, the money could be well spent if it led to a general improvement in what is widely seen as an inadequate national public health infrastructure.

Anthrax, though a potential killer, is not spread from person to person and can be effectively treated by available antibiotics. Smallpox, which is communicable and untreatable, would be worse. If smallpox or some other agent appears, who will detect and identify it quickly? Who will know where to access even the limited supplies of vaccine? Who will decide who will be vaccinated? We need open, nationwide information systems and live or machine monitors that can discern relevant patterns. Local expertise will be essential, as will biologists, medical personnel, and information technologists who can devise and use the kinds of systems that make slight patterns discernible. The magnitude of the challenge is apparent in a very recent report from the Institute of Medicine that systematically analyzes the strengths and weaknesses of the Metropolitan Medical Response System Program. Initiated when such attacks seemed to be thought experiments, the report was completed after September 11. Perhaps someone will pay more than modest attention to it because it is dedicated to one of the expert committee members, Raymond M. Downey, chief of rescue operations in the Fire Department of New York City, who died in the line of duty at the World Trade Center.

As important as paying serious attention to available information is new research that might allow for more rapid detection and treatment of known and unknown agents of chemical and biological warfare. Broadly knowledgeable people from university and industrial laboratories can inform government officials about relevant, innovative work that deserves support. A reordering of priorities for the grant programs at the NSF and NIH in favor of these new concerns needs consideration. For example, several recent scientific reports suggest new approaches to treatments for anthrax. Perhaps these studies should be put on a fast track. As new therapies and vaccines come into view, it may be well to recall two principles that Vannevar Bush established for the OSRD.

First, the OSRD maintained that a new device didn't need to be perfect to be adopted. The proximity fuse, for example, went into production in late 1942, only two years after the British gave the idea to the OSRD. At the time, only 52 percent of these radio-controlled detonators turned out by a pilot production line worked, that is, were able to explode a shell near a target rather than after a fixed time or on impact. The success rate increased significantly by the end of the war when 70,000 of the fingertip-sized devices were produced per day and quickly sent to both the Pacific and Atlantic war theaters for use against aircraft and missiles. Second, the OSRD considered time to application highly relevant; devices likely to come on line only after the war was over were not pursued. Now, for example, the FDA may need to expedite and revise its usual procedures to hasten the availability of relevant vaccines and therapies if we cannot await full-scale clinical trials or ethically test in the absence of diseased people (e.g., smallpox). Drugs or vaccines that work in only 50 percent of the people could save a lot of lives as long as they are safe, and in extreme situations, safety itself could become relative.

Computers and their potential were just emerging as World War II began. Bush himself was a significant pioneer in the development of analog computers and consequently biased against the developing digital approaches. He had even been thinking about a machine he called the "memex" that, with its viewing screen and keyboard, would make the knowledge of the ages available to all. But when in 1940 the OSRD decided not to support Norbert Wiener's proposal for developing digital systems, it was because Bush did not believe that a useful machine could be produced in time to help the war effort and the project would therefore waste precious human and financial resources. Now, digital machines are integral to our national infrastructure and personal lives, and a target for professional pranksters and terrorists.

One way or another, our government, military, financial transactions, power, fuels, water, transportation, and businesses all now depend on computer data banks and networks. An attack on any one of these could spell widespread disruption of everyday life in the U.S. Consider what a hacker's virus does to an office network. Imagine instead the consequences of stopping the New York City subways or the Washington Metro. Unlike biological or chemical attacks, which are difficult to protect against, there are preventive strategies against "information warfare," as it has been called.

As with bioterrorism, information warfare's basic features are described in various largely ignored authoritative reports and include low cost; availability to both individuals and nations; the difficulty of distinguishing terrorists from troublemaking hackers, accidents, or espionage; and the irrelevancy of geographical distance that makes targets in the U.S. vulnerable from anywhere in the world. The need for expert technical attention is emphasized in a RAND report statement that "the subject matter is very new and, in some dimensions, technically complex, especially for individuals typically found in policy making positions."

There was a time when DARPA had access to the most advanced thinking about computers. In the 1960s, its support of information technology was the driving force behind the development of the internet and associated early work on other innovative computer techniques. This was accomplished through consistent support of free-ranging, revolutionary basic research by outstanding people at universities. Then, in the early 1970s, just as the internet was taking off, DARPA changed policies and began restricting its support to projects defined by the Pentagon agenda. By 1986, civilian technical leaders no longer staffed the critical DARPA office. Although it was ultimately dropped, a further chill on the connections between the Pentagon and the scientific community resulted from the Mansfield Amendment in the 1970s, which required that the Defense Department support only that basic research that had a direct relation to military needs. This was equivalent to saying that no basic research would be supported by the Pentagon because by definition, basic research is without specific goals except to advance knowledge in a particular field.

The further development of the internet and other sophisticated tools for building powerful databases, communications networks, pattern recognition techniques and such technologies occurred in the private sector. It is not clear whether the Department of Defense now can match the technology in the scientific and industrial communities or has access to smart, unconventional people like those who built the great information technology companies. Perhaps patriotism and the recent demise of some of the start-up companies will encourage such people to work on national problems.

Though chilling to think about, the number and variety of possible terrorist devices and actions are large. At the same time that we plan to detect and defend against more obvious possible attacks on civilians, research is also needed in other areas. Examples include remote sensing from space, aviation security, alternative fuels, explosives detection and control and home and workplace building safety.

With the exception of its attention to the psychiatric problems that were the largest reason for medical discharge during the war, the OSRD paid minimal heed to the social sciences or humanities. But it is already clear from the ramified effects of the September 11 attack and subsequent anthrax dispersal that our nation would benefit from attention to existing knowledge and the encouragement of additional research in, for example, economics, mass psychology, and Islamic cultures.

We have all been surprised by the multiple profound effects of a single day's terror on our national economy. It is not obvious that our government had made a serious previous effort to study the possible economic ramifications of attacks within the U.S. or what ameliorating steps might be taken. Such thinking could be of great consequence to everything from small businesses to large corporations. A web search turned up only one study of the costs of anthrax, brucellosis and tularemia epidemics. In short, we're unprepared for the staggering economic, as well as security, implications of these attacks.

From the beginning of the current crisis, the citizenry has looked to the national government for clarification of inherently ambiguous media reports. We are instead only advised to be wary but at the same time go about our normal lives. But many people are anxious and some near panic. Thoughtful social scientists could help devise honest and constructive ways to lead the nation through this situation and the worse ones that may ensue.

It is impossible to imagine all possible terrorist threats. Scholars of science fiction could probably provide more scenarios than an officialdom limited by mainstream thinking. And of the threats that seem likely, which ones should we be prepared for? In the event of a large-scale attack, how do we decide who gets priority for treatment? There is a need to engage those who have modeled epidemics or have thought deeply about how to analyze risk.

4.

The nation will be better off if it reaches out to gather even the off-the-wall ideas that scholars, scientists, and engineers can provide. Sharing those ideas among government agencies will more likely occur if the federal focus on innovation is not located within an existing bureaucracy. The new Office of Homeland Security, based as it is in the White House, can take the leadership in this, although it will require of Governor Tom Ridge, the head of the new office, the same sort of brash, insistent effort that Vannevar Bush made. He should also be given a hard-charging scientist as his deputy. This organization, independent from established government agencies, as was the OSRD, could be an efficient way to marshal expert advice for the challenge of terrorism.

Too often, strategic plans for government programs fail to address one question critical to their success: are there highly trained, skilled, and competent people available to carry out and sustain the program? It is assumed, and hiring rules often support such assumptions, that it is good enough to hire the most highly qualified person available and rely on "training" courses to bring marginally qualified people up to snuff. Now, the U.S. defense and intelligence agencies must recruit the very best people regardless of political views. Those in power need to accept that they can never emulate the imaginations, facile talents and up-to-date knowledge of even unconventional young people. Vannevar Bush constantly sought draft deferments for people he thought essential—and almost all of them were less than 26 years old. Outstanding scientists, engineers, and scholars are often independent and nonconformist while military and bureaucratic minds are more tuned to rules and regimentation. The histories of the OSRD, the early years of DARPA, NASA, and the NIH tell us that there are productive ways to promote interaction between these very different worlds both within the government and by outreach of government to universities and industry. The OSRD's policy of letting people work wherever they were rather than gathering them into government labs and offices is likely to still be most efficient.

International terrorism and the need for smart, responsive strategies are likely to be with us for a long time. Our future security will require a constant supply of people trained in math, science, engineering, and serious computer science. Yet at present, diminishing numbers of young Americans enter these fields. Endless numbers of reports and a lot of money for K–12 education have tried and failed to address this situation. In recent years, of doctoral degrees awarded by U.S. institutions, about a third in science and half in engineering went to foreigners. Many of those students will remain in the U.S. and contribute to our needs. We welcome them, but also realize that the expertise of those from poor countries could, if they returned home, help ameliorate the conditions that support terrorism.

Building the scientific research infrastructure in developing countries can lead directly to improved economies, health care, and general living conditions. The U.S. scientific community has important roles to play in this endeavor. One path is through its typical and extensive informal networks. Another is through formal mechanisms such as the international network of National Academies of Science initiated by the president of the U.S. Academy. A third, the establishment of world-class laboratories in developing countries, has been discouraging in the past because the laboratories are frequently unsustainable when the international sponsoring organization leaves. It is difficult to convince the host countries that investment in a scientific and engineering infrastructure, including trained scientists and engineers, should have priority because of its long-term effect on improving daily life. New approaches are needed.

It will be especially challenging to enhance scientific interactions within Muslim countries, especially those in which government and religion are either unified or intertwined and whose hostility to the U.S. is, at least partly, the consequence of distrust of our technological advances. Professor Seyyid Hossein Nasr, a professor of Islamic studies at George Washington University, believes "that the cultural crisis created by the successful introduction of Western science and technology, successful enough to bring about rapid cultural patterns of change, is going to continue to pose major problems for the Islamic world." Perhaps experience with similar conflicts at home between scientists and people of fundamentalist faiths can help direct us toward constructive conversations with scientists in Islamic nations.

Millions of people in poor nations watch their children die of diseases we have not seen in generations. They themselves are likely to suffer without hope of medical care from malaria, AIDS, tuberculosis, cholera, and other diseases. (Estimates of annual deaths from malaria worldwide were recently raised from 1 million to 2.7 million.) To such people, the introduction of dangerous biological and chemical agents into our relatively clean environments may not seem as horrible as it does to us. Also, the willingness of terrorists to die for a cause we find unfathomable may be influenced by the fact that life spans in their societies are in any case short. We need to see the world as our enemies do if we are to defend ourselves successfully. We have known for a long time of the tremendous disparity between the health of our populations and of those in developing countries. We have avoided doing much about this because our policies have been driven by free-market concepts and a miserly concept of our national wealth. Now we are forced to spend tens of billions of dollars of that wealth recuperating from and preparing for terrorist acts. Threatened people might now be less aggrieved if we had used those same tens of billions to share with them the things that give us such healthy lives, just as we shared with a devastated Europe at the end of World

War II through the Marshall Plan. Sound arguments can certainly be made that this is not really our responsibility, but it
may be more constructive to recognize that finding ways to
share our medical technology is an integral part of national
defense in this new era.

INDEX